The Blessings of
CHRISTMAS

The Blessings of
CHRISTMAS

IDEALS PUBLICATIONS INCORPORATED
NASHVILLE, TENNESSEE

ISBN 0-8249-4034-2

Printed and bound in the U.S.A. by R.R. Donnelly & Sons, Willard, Ohio.

Library of Congress Cataloging-in-Publication Data
The Blessings of Christmas.
      p.   cm.
    Includes index.
    ISBN 0-8249-4034-2 (alk. paper)
    1. Christmas stories. 2. Christmas--Poetry. I. Ideals
Publications Incorporated.
PN6071.C6B52 1998
820'.0334--dc21
                                     98-44457
                                           CIP

First Edition
10 8 6 4 2 1 3 5 7 9

Publisher, Patricia A. Pingry
Designer, Eve DeGrie
Assistant Designer, Catherine Fet
Copy Editor, Kristi Richardson

Color Film Separations by Precision Color Graphics, New Berlin, Wisconsin.

Published by Ideals Publications Incorporated
535 Metroplex Drive, Suite 250
Nashville, TN 37211

Cover photograph: Nativity Window, copyright The Crosiers, Gene Plaisted, OSC.
Photograph on page two: Nativity Star, Corpus Christi Church, Bismarck, North Dakota, copyright The Crosiers, Gene Plaisted, OSC.
Photograph on page three: Country living room decorated for Christmas Eve, copyright Jessie Walker Associates.

ACKNOWLEDGMENTS

BINNS, ELSIE, "The Smallest Angel." Copyright © 1942 by Story Parade. Reprinted with permission. BISHOP, JIM, "The Holy Birth." Reprinted with the permission of Simon & Schuster from The Book of Jesus by Calvin Miller. Copyright © 1996 by Calvin Miller. BROUN, HEYWOOD, "Frankincense and Myrrh" and "Inasmuch." From Collected Edition of Heywood Broun. Used with the permission of the Estate of Heywood Broun. CARMICHAEL, AMY, "A Carol." From Toward Jerusalem by Amy Carmichael, copyright © 1977. Reprinted with the permission of Christian Literature Crusade. COATSWORTH, ELIZABETH, "After Christmas a Landlord Remembers." Reprinted with the permission of Simon & Schuster Books for Young Readers, an imprint of Simon & Schuster Children's Publishing Division. From Country Poems by Elizabeth Coatsworth. Copyright © 1942 by Elizabeth Coatsworth; copyright renewed. COLUM, PADRAIC, "A Cradle Song." From Poems by Padraic Colum. Reprinted with the permission of the Estate of Padraic Colum. DE LA MARE, WALTER, "A Ballad of Christmas." Used by permission of The Literary Trustees of Walter de la Mare, and the Society of Authors as their representative. FARRAR, GERALDINE, "The Little Christmas Donkey." Copyright © 1938 by Carl Fischer, Inc. Copyright renewed. International Copyright Secured. Reprinted by permission. GORDON, ARTHUR, "The Miraculous Staircase." Reprinted with the permission of Guideposts Magazine. HOLMES, MARJORIE, "In Praise of Christmas Letters," copyright © 1991 and "At Christmas the Heart Goes Home" copyright © 1976 by Guideposts Magazine. Reprinted with permission. JAQUES, EDNA, "The Lighted Candle." From Beside Still Waters by Edna Jaques, copyright © 1952 in Canada by Thomas Allen & Son Limited. Reprinted with permission. MARSHALL, PETER, "Christmas Grace" [Friday, December 19, 1947], "For Christmas the Year Round," "Christmas Prayer," and "The Day after Christmas." From The Prayers of Peter Marshall, edited by Catherine Marshall. Copyright © 1949, 1950, 1951, 1954 and 1982. Used by permission of Chosen Books, a division of Baker Book House. McGINLEY, PHYLLIS, "Christmas Eve in Our Village" and "Lady Selecting Her Christmas Cards." From Merry Christmas, Happy New Year by Phyllis McGinley. Copyright © 1958. Reprinted with permission. NATHAN, ROBERT, "To Come Unto Me." Used with permission. PARKER, DOROTHY, "The Maid-servant at the Inn." From The Portable Dorothy Parker by Dorothy Parker. Copyright © 1928, renewed © 1956 by Dorothy Parker. Used by permission of Viking Penguin, a division of Penguin Putnam Inc. STRONG, PATIENCE, "Homesick" © from The House of Dreams, "The Star" © from Wayside Glory, "The Stable Door" © from Wayside Altars. Reprinted with the permission of Rupert Crew Limited. STRUTHER, JAN, "Three Stockings," from Mrs. Miniver, copyright 1940 by Jan Struther and renewed 1967 by J.A. Maxtone Graham, reprinted by permission of Harcourt Brace & Company. VAN DYKE, HENRY, "A Christmas Prayer for the Home." Reprinted with the permission of Simon & Schuster from The Book of Jesus by Calvin Miller. Copyright © 1996 by Calvin Miller. WAUGH, EVELYN, "To the Three Kings." Reprinted by permission of The Peters Fraser and Dunlop Group Limited, on behalf of Evelyn Waugh. From Helena by Evelyn Waugh. Copyright © 1950.

Table of CONTENTS

Blessings of HOME

Homesick

Patience Strong

God bless all the homesick
As they dream of some dear place,
The home they left behind them,
Good old friends, a mother's face.
Such thoughts come back, just little things
Remembered suddenly,
The chair beside the kitchen grate,
The cat, the hawthorn tree,
The best blue teacups on the shelf,
The rustic garden seat,
The knocker on the old front door,
The quiet, familiar street.

A hundred things drift back
Across the chasm of the years,
A hundred things that tear the heart
And fill the eyes with tears.
God comfort them! And in their yearning,
May they realize,
Christ came, not for the arrogant
Or for the worldly wise,
But for the weak and weary
On Life's troubled tempest tossed,
The homesick and the hunted,
And the lonely and the lost.

A cozy home at Christmastime. Photograph copyright Jessie Walker Associates.

A Christmas Prayer FOR THE HOME

Henry Van Dyke

Father of all men, look upon our family,
Kneeling together before thee,
And grant us a true Christmas.

With loving hearts we bless Thee:
> For the gift of Thy dear Son Jesus Christ,
> For the peace He brings to human homes,
> For the good will He teaches to sinful men,
> For the glory of Thy goodness shining in His face.

With joyful voice we praise Thee:
> For His lowly birth and His rest in the manger,
> For the pure tenderness of His mother Mary,
> For the fatherly care that protected Him,
> For the providence that saved the Holy child
> To be the Saviour of the world.

With deep desire we beseech Thee:
> Help us to keep His birthday truly,
> Help us to offer, in His name, our Christmas prayer.
> From the sickness of sin and the darkness of doubt,
> From the selfish pleasures and sullen pains,
> From the frost of pride and the fever of envy,
> God save us every one, through the blessing of Jesus.

In the health of purity and the calm of mutual trust,
In the sharing of joy and the bearing of trouble,
In the steady glow of love and the clear light of hope,
God keep us every one, by the blessing of Jesus.

In praying and praising, in giving and receiving,
In eating and drinking, in singing and making merry,
In parents' gladness and in children's mirth,
In dear memories of those who have departed,
In good comradeship with those who are here,
In kind wishes for those who are far away,
In patient waiting, sweet contentment, generous cheer,
God bless us every one, with the blessing of Jesus.

A warm and inviting kitchen welcomes the Christmas guests.
Photograph copyright Jessie Walker Associates.

By remembering our kinship with all men,
By well-wishing, friendly speaking and kindly doing,
By cheering the downcast and adding sunshine to daylight,
By welcoming strangers (poor shepherds or wise men),
By keeping the music of the angels' song in this home,
God help us every one to share the blessing of Jesus:

In whose name we keep Christmas,
And whose words we pray together:

Our Father, which art in heaven, hallowed by Thy name,
Thy kingdom come. Thy will be done in earth, as it is in heaven.
Give us this day our daily bread. And forgive us our debts, as we forgive our debtors.
And lead us not into temptation, but deliver us from evil:
For Thine is the kingdom, and the power, and the glory, forever. Amen.

At Christmas the HEART GOES HOME

Marjorie Holmes

At Christmas all roads lead home.

The filled planes, packed trains, and overflowing buses all speak eloquently of a single destination: home. Despite the crowding and the crushing, the delays, the confusion, we clutch our bright packages and beam our anticipation. We are like birds driven by an instinct we only faintly understand—the hunger to be with our own people.

If we are already snug by our own fireside, surrounded by growing children, or awaiting the return of older ones who are away, then the heart takes a side trip. In memory we journey back to the Christmases of long ago. Once again we are curled into quivering balls of excitement, listening to the mysterious rustle of tissue paper and the tinkle of untold treasures as parents perform their magic on Christmas Eve. Or we recall the special Christmases that are like little landmarks in the life of a family.

One memory is particularly dear to me—a Christmas during the Great Depression when Dad was out of work and the rest of us were scattered, struggling to get through school or simply to survive. My sister Gwen and her schoolteacher husband, on his first job in another state, were expecting their first baby. My brother Harold, an aspiring actor, was traveling with a road show. I was a senior working my way through a small college five hundred miles away. My boss had offered me fifty dollars—a fortune!—just to keep the office open the two weeks he and his wife would be gone.

"And boy, do I need the money. Mom, I know you'll understand," I wrote.

I wasn't prepared for her brave if wistful reply. The other kids couldn't make it either. Except for my kid brother Barney, she and Dad would be alone. "This house is going to seem empty, but don't worry— we'll be okay."

I did worry, though. Our first Christmas apart! And as the carols drifted up the stairs, as the corridors rang with the laughter and chatter of other girls packing up to leave, my misery deepened.

Then one night when the dorm was almost empty I had a long distance call. "Gwen!" I gasped. "What's wrong?" (Long distance usually meant an emergency back in those days.)

"Listen, Leon's got a new generator and we think the old jalopy can make it home. I've wired Harold—if he can meet us halfway, he can ride with us. But don't tell the folks; we want to surprise them. Marj, you've just got to come too."

"But I haven't got a dime for presents."

"Neither have we. Cut up a catalog and bring pictures of all the goodies you'd buy if you could—and will someday!"

"I could do *that*, Gwen. But I just can't leave here now."

When we hung up I reached for the scissors. Furs and perfume. Wristwatches, clothes, cars—how all of us longed to lavish beautiful things on those we loved. Well, at least I could mail mine home—with IOUs.

I was still dreaming over this wish list when I was called to the phone again. It was my boss, saying he'd decided to close the office after all. My heart leaped up, for if it wasn't too late to catch a ride as far as Fort Dodge with the girl down the hall—I ran to pound on her door.

They already had a load, she said—but if I was willing to sit on somebody's lap. . . . Her dad was downstairs waiting. I threw things into a suitcase, then rammed a hand down the torn lining of my coat sleeve so fast it emerged mittened and I had to start over.

It was snowing as we piled into that heaterless car. We drove all night with the side curtains flapping, singing and hugging each other to keep warm. Not minding—how could we? We were going home! . . .

"Marj!" Mother stood at the door, clutching her robe about her, silver-black hair spilling down her back, eyes large with alarm, then incredulous joy. "Oh . . . *Marj*."

I'll never forget those eyes or the feel of her arms around me, so soft and warm after the bitter cold. My feet felt frozen after that all-night drive, but they warmed up as my parents fed me and put me to bed. And when I woke up hours later, it was to the jangle of the sleigh bells Dad hung on the door

This painting by P. Grim illustrates the tradition of bringing home the Christmas tree. Photograph copyright Superstock.

each year. And voices. My kid brother shouting, "Harold! Gwen!" The clamor of astonished greetings, the laughter, the kissing, the questions. And we all gathered around the kitchen table the way we used to, recounting our adventures.

"I had to hitchhike clear to Peoria," my older brother scolded merrily. "*Me*, the leading man!" He lifted an elegant two-toned shoe—with a flapping sole—"In these!"

"But by golly, you got here." Dad's chubby face was beaming. Then suddenly he broke down—Dad, who never cried. "We're together!"

Together. The best present we could give one another, we realized. All of us. Just being here in the old house where we'd shared so many Christmases. No gifts on our lavish lists, if they could materialize, could equal that. . . .

In most Christmases since that memorable one we've been lucky. During the years our children were growing up there were no separations. Then one year, appallingly, history repeated itself. For valid reasons, not a single faraway child could get home. Worse, my husband had flown to Florida for some vital surgery. A proud, brave man—he was adamant about our not coming with him "just because it's Christmas" when he'd be back in another week.

Like my mother before me, I still had one lone chick left—Melanie, fourteen. "We'll get along fine," she said, trying to cheer me.

We built a big fire every evening, went to church, wrapped presents, pretended. But the ache in our hearts kept swelling. And the day before Christmas we burst into mutual tears. "Mommy, it's just not right for Daddy to be down there alone!"

"I know it." Praying for a miracle, I ran to the telephone. The airlines were hopeless, but there was one roomette available on the last train to Miami. Almost hysterical with relief, we threw things into bags.

And what a Christmas Eve! Excited as conspirators, we cuddled together in that cozy space. Melanie hung a tiny wreath in the window and we settled down to watch the endless pageantry flashing by to the rhythmic clicking song of the rails: little villages and city streets—all dancing with lights and decorations and sparkling Christmas trees; and cars and snowy countrysides and people—all the people. Each one on his or her special pilgrimage of love and celebration this precious night.

At last we drifted off to sleep. But hours later I awoke to a strange stillness. The train had stopped. And, raising the shade, I peered out on a very small town. Silent, deserted, with only a few lights still burning. And under the bare branches, along a lonely street, a figure was walking. A young man in sailor blues, head bent, hunched under the weight of the sea bag on his shoulders. And I thought—*home! Poor kid, he's almost home.* And I wondered if there was someone still up waiting for him; or if anyone knew he

was coming at all. And my heart cried out to him, for he was suddenly my own son—and my own ghost, and the soul of us all—driven, so immutably driven by this annual call, "Come home!"

Home for Christmas. There must be some deep psychological reason why we turn so instinctively toward home at this special time. Perhaps we are acting out the ancient story of a man and a woman and a coming child, plodding along with their donkey

toward their destination. . . .

The child who was born on that first Christmas grew up to be a man. Jesus. He healed many people, taught us many important things. But the message that has left the most lasting impression and given the most hope and comfort is this: We do have a home to go to, and there will be an ultimate homecoming. A place where we will indeed be reunited with those we love.

Anyway, that's my idea of Heaven. A place where Mother is standing in the door, probably bossing Dad the way she used to about the turkey or the tree, and he's enjoying every minute of it. And old friends and neighbors are streaming in and out and the sense of love and joy and celebration will go on forever.

A place where every day will be Christmas, with everybody there together. At home.

A painting by an unknown artist captures the joyful gathering on Christmas day. Photograph copyright Superstock.

A Rocking Hymn

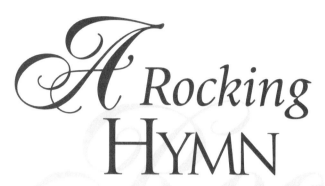

George Wither

Sweet baby, sleep! What ails my dear?
What ails my darling thus to cry?
Be still, my child, and lend thine ear
To hear me sing thy lullaby.
My pretty lamb, forbear to weep;
Be still, my dear; sweet baby, sleep!

When God with us was dwelling here,
In little babes He took delight;
Such innocents as thou, my dear,
Are ever precious in His sight.
Sweet baby, then, forbear to weep;
Be still, my babe; sweet baby, sleep!

A little Infant once was He,
And strength in weakness then was laid
Upon His virgin-mother's knee,

That power to thee might be conveyed.
Sweet baby, then, forbear to weep;
Be still, my babe; sweet baby, sleep!

In this thy frailty and thy need
He friends and helpers doth prepare,
Which thee shall cherish, clothe, and feed,
For of thy weal they tender are.
Sweet baby, then, forbear to weep!
Be still, my babe; sweet baby, sleep.

The King of kings, when He was born,
Had not so much for outward ease;
By Him such dressings were not worn,
Nor such like swaddling clothes as these.
Sweet baby, then, forbear to weep!
Be still, my babe; sweet baby, sleep.

Within a manger lodged thy Lord,
Where oxen lay and asses fed;
Warm rooms we do to thee afford,
An easy cradle or a bed.
My baby, then, forbear to weep;
Be still, my babe; sweet baby, sleep!

Thou hast, yet more, to perfect this,
A promise and an earnest got
Of gaining everlasting bliss,
Though thou, my babe, perceiv'st it not.
Sweet baby, then, forbear to weep;
Be still, my babe; sweet baby, sleep.

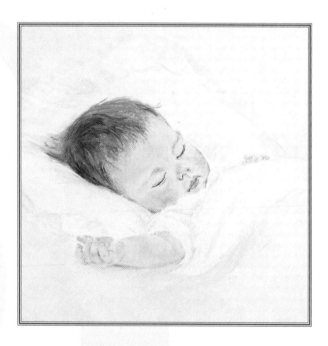

A sleeping baby by artist Frances Hook. Painting copyright Ideals Publications Incorporated.

Painting by Russ Flint depicting Mary and the Baby Jesus.
Copyright Ideals Publications Incorporated.

A Christmas GRACE

Peter Marshall

We thank Thee, O God, for the return of the wondrous spell of this Christmas season that brings its own sweet joy into our jaded and troubled hearts.

Forbid it, Lord, that we should celebrate without understanding what we celebrate, or, like our counterparts so long ago, fail to see the star or to hear the song of glorious promise.

As our hearts yield to the spirit of Christmas, may we discover that it is Thy Holy Spirit who comes—not a sentiment, but a power—to remind us of the only way by which there may be peace on the earth and good will among men.

May we not spend Christmas, but keep it, that we may be kept in its hope, through Him who emptied Himself in coming to us that we might be filled with peace and joy in returning to God. Amen.

The Christmas baking has begun in this warm kitchen.
Photograph copyright Jessie Walker Associates.

What Christmas Is
As We Grow Older

Charles Dickens

Time was, with most of us, when Christmas Day encircled all our limited world like a magic ring, left nothing out for us to miss or seek; bound together all our home enjoyments, affections, and hopes; grouped everything and every one around the Christmas fire; and made the little picture shining in our bright young eyes complete.

Time came, perhaps, all too soon, when our thoughts overleaped that narrow boundary; when there was some one (very dear, we thought then, very beautiful, and absolutely perfect) wanting to the fullness of our happiness; when we were wanting too (or we thought so, which did just as well) at the Christmas hearth by which that some one sat; and when we intertwined with every wreath and garland of our life that some one's name.

That was the time for the bright visionary Christmases which have long arisen from us to show faintly, after summer rain, in the palest edges of the rainbow! That was the time for the beatified enjoyment of the things that were to be, and never were, and yet the things that were so real in our resolute hope that it would be hard to say, now, what realities achieved since, have been stronger!

What! Did that Christmas never really come when we and the priceless pearl who was our young choice were received, after the happiest of totally impossible marriages, by the two united families previously at daggers-drawn on our account? When brothers and sisters-in-law who had always been rather cool to us before our relationship was effected, perfectly doted on us, and when fathers and mothers overwhelmed us with unlimited incomes? Was that Christmas dinner never really eaten, after which we arose, and generously and eloquently rendered honour to our late rival, present in the company, then and there exchanging friendship and forgiveness, and founding an attachment, not to be surpassed in Greek or Roman story, which subsisted until death? Has that same rival long ceased to care for that same priceless pearl, and married for money, and become usurious? Above all, do we really know, now, that we should probably have been miserable if we had won and worn the pearl, and that we are better without her?

That Christmas when we had recently achieved so much fame; when we had been carried in triumph somewhere, for doing something great and good; when we had won an honoured and ennobled name, and arrived and were received at home in a shower of tears of joy; is it possible that *that* Christmas has not come yet?

And is our life here, at the best, so constituted that, pausing as we advance at such a noticeable milestone in the track as this great birthday, we look back on the things that never were, as naturally and full as gravely as on the things that have been and are gone, or have been and still are? If it be so, and so it seems to be, must we come to the conclusion that life is little better than a dream, and little worth the loves and strivings that we crowd into it?

No! Far be such miscalled philosophy from us, dear Reader, on Christmas Day! Nearer and closer to our hearts be the Christmas spirit, which is the spirit of active usefulness, perseverance, cheerful discharge of duty, kindness and forbearance! It is in the last virtues especially, that we are, or should be, strengthened by the unaccomplished visions of our youth; for, who shall say that they are not our teachers to deal gently even with the impalpable nothings of the earth!

Therefore, as we grow older, let us be more thankful that the circle of our Christmas associations and of the lessons that they bring, expands! Let us welcome every one of them, and summon them to take their places by the Christmas hearth.

Welcome, old aspirations, glittering creatures of an ardent fancy, to your shelter underneath the holly! We know you, and have not outlived you yet. Welcome, old projects and old loves, however fleeting, to your nooks among the steadier lights that burn around us. Welcome, all that was ever real to our hearts; and for the earnestness that made you real, thanks to Heaven! Do we build no Christmas castles in the clouds now? Let your thoughts, fluttering like butterflies among these flowers of children, bear witness! Before this boy, there stretches out a Future,

brighter than we ever looked on in our old romantic time, but bright with honour and with truth. Around this little head on which the sunny curls lie heaped, the graces sport, as prettily, as airily, as when there was no scythe within the reach of Time to shear away the curls of our first love. Upon another girl's face near it—placider but smiling bright—a quiet and contented little face, we see Home fairly written. Shining from the word, as rays shine from a star, we see how, when our graves are old, other hopes than ours are young, other hearts than ours are moved; how other ways are smoothed; how other happiness blooms, ripens, and decays—no, not decays, for other homes and other bands of children, not yet in being nor for ages yet to be, arise, and bloom and ripen to the end of all!

Welcome, everything! Welcome, alike what has been, and what never was, and what we hope may be, to your shelter underneath the holly, to your places round the Christmas fire, where what is sits open-hearted! In yonder shadow, do we see obtruding furtively upon the blaze, an enemy's face? By Christmas Day we do forgive him! If the injury he has done us may admit of such companionship, let him come here and take his place. If otherwise, unhappily, let him go hence, assured that we will never injure nor accuse him.

On this day we shut out Nothing!

"Pause," says a low voice. "Nothing? Think!"

"On Christmas Day, we will shut out from our fireside, Nothing."

"Not the shadow of a vast City where the withered leaves are lying deep?" the voice replies. "Not the shadow that darkens the whole globe? Not the shadow of the City of the Dead?"

Not even that. Of all days in the year, we will turn our faces towards that City upon Christmas Day, and from its silent hosts bring those we loved among us. City of the Dead, in the blessed name wherein we are gathered together at this time, and in the Presence that is here among us according to the promise, we will receive, and not dismiss, the people who are dear to us!

Yes. We can look upon these children angels that alight, so solemnly, so beautifully among the living children by the fire, and can bear to think how they departed from us. Entertaining angels unawares, as the Patriarchs did, the playful children are unconscious of their guests; but we can see them—can see a radiant arm around one favourite neck, as if there were a tempting of that child away. Among the celestial figures there is one, a poor misshapen boy on earth, of a glorious beauty now, of whom his dying mother said it grieved her much to leave him here, alone, for so many years as it was likely would elapse before he came to her—being such a little child. But he went quickly, and was laid upon her breast, and in her hand she leads him.

There was a gallant boy, who fell, far away, upon a burning sand beneath a burning sun, and said, "Tell them at home, with my last love, how much I could have wished to kiss them once, but that I died, contented and had done my duty!" Or there was another, over whom they read the words, "Therefore we commit his body to the deep," and so consigned him to the lonely ocean and sailed on. Or there was another, who lay down to his rest in the dark shadow of great forests, and, on earth, awoke no more. Oh, shall they not, from sand and sea and forest, be brought home at such a time?

We had a friend who was our friend from early days, with whom we often pictured the changes that were to come upon our lives, and merrily imagined how we would speak, and walk, and think, and talk, when we came to be old. His destined habita-

tion in the City of the Dead received him in his prime. Shall he be shut out from our Christmas remembrance? Would his love have so excluded us? Lost friend, lost child, lost parent, sister, brother, husband, wife, we will not so discard you! You shall hold your cherished places in our Christmas hearts, and by our Christmas fires; and in the season of immortal hope, and on the birthday of immortal mercy, we will shut out Nothing!

The winter sun goes down over town and village; on the sea it makes a rosy path, as if the Sacred tread were fresh upon the water.

A few more moments, and it sinks, and night comes on, and lights begin to sparkle in the prospect. On the hillside beyond the shapelessly diffused town, and in the quiet keeping of the trees that gird the village steeple, remembrances are cut in stone, planted in common flowers, growing in grass, entwined with lowly brambles around many a mound of earth. In town and village, there are doors and windows closed against the weather, there are flaming logs heaped high, there are joyful faces, there is healthy music of voices. Be all ungentleness and harm excluded from the temples of the Household Gods, but be those remembrances admitted with tender encouragement! They are of the time and all its comforting and peaceful reassurances; and of the history that reunited even upon earth the living and the dead; and of the broad beneficence and goodness that too many men have tried to tear to narrow shreds.

A beautiful sunrise over the icy bay of Acadia National Park along the coast of Maine. Photograph copyright Johnson's Photography.

Blessings of FAMILY

The Lighted Candle

Edna Jaques

I have no window looking on the street,
Where I might set a candle Christmas Eve,
To light the little Jesus on His way,
For it is said . . . and so I do believe
The little Christ child walks again on earth,
On this sweet-memoried evening of His birth.

My window looks upon a little lane
Where there are rutted tracks and broken things:
An old gray shed . . . a bit of sagging fence,
So poor, and yet tonight the moonlight flings
A shining banner like a silver haze,
Clothing with beauty all its shabby ways.

And so perhaps if He should come our way
Along this little frozen path, He might
See beauty in a humble country lane.
So I will pull the curtains back tonight,
And set a candle where its flickering glow
Will make a path of silver in the snow.

A New Hampshire home is gaily decorated to welcome friends and family with luminarias, which are candles placed in weighted paper bags. Photograph copyright Johnson's Photography.

A Prayer—
for Christmas the YEAR ROUND

Peter Marshall

Lord Jesus, we thank Thee for the spirit shed abroad in human hearts on Christmas. Even as we invited Thee on Christmas to be born again in our hearts, so wilt Thou now go with us throughout the days ahead, to be our Companion in all that we do. Wilt Thou help each one of us to keep Christmas alive in our hearts and in our homes, that it may continue to glow, to shed its warmth, to speak its message during all the bleak days of winter.

May we hold to that spirit, that we may be as gentle and as kindly today as we were on Christmas Eve, as generous tomorrow as we were on Christmas morning.

Then if—by Thy help—we should live through a whole week in that spirit, it may be we can go into another week, and thus be encouraged and gladdened by the discovery that Christmas can last the year round.

So give us joyful, cheerful hearts to the glory of Jesus Christ, our Lord. Amen.

Painting by Marion Quimby offers a traditional village at Christmastime.

Christmas
TREASURES

Eugene Field

I count my treasures o'er with care,
    The little toy my darling knew,
    A little sock of faded hue,
A little lock of golden hair.

Long years ago this holy time,
    My little one—my all to me—
    Sat robed in white upon my knee
And heard the merry Christmas chime.

"Tell me, my little golden-head,
    If Santa Claus should come tonight,
    What shall he bring my baby bright,—
What treasure for my boy?" I said.

And then he named this little toy,
    While in his round and mournful eyes
    There came a look of sweet surprise,
That spoke his quiet, trustful joy.

And as he lisped his evening prayer
    He asked the boon with childish grace,
    Then, toddling to the chimney place,
He hung his little stocking there.

That night, while lengthening shadows crept,
    I saw the white-robed angels come
    With singing to our lowly home
And kiss my darling as he slept.

They must have heard his little prayer,
    For in the morn, with rapturous face,
    He toddled to the chimney-place,
And found this little treasure there.

They came again one Christmas-tide,—
    That angel host, so fair and white!
    And singing all that glorious night,
They lured my darling from my side.

A little sock, a little toy,
    A little lock of golden hair,
    The Christmas music on the air,
A watching for my baby boy!

But if again that angel train
    And golden-head come back for me,
    To bear me to Eternity,
My watching will not be in vain!

A little boy hugs his new Christmas toy in this oil painting.
Copyright Ideals Publications Incorporated.

Learning the Truth of
THE CHRISTMAS SPIRIT

Louisa May Alcott

"I'm so tired of Christmas I wish there never would be another one!" exclaimed a discontented-looking little girl, as she sat idly watching her mother arrange a pile of gifts two days before they were to be given.

"Why, Effie, what a dreadful thing to say! Why are you tired of what should be the happiest time of all the year?" asked Mamma, anxiously.

"Perhaps I shouldn't be if I had something new. But it is always the same, and there isn't any more surprise about it. I always find heaps of goodies in my stocking. Don't like some of them, and soon get tired of those I do like. We always have a great dinner, and I eat too much, and feel ill next day. Then there is a Christmas tree somewhere, with a doll on top, or a stupid old Santa Claus, and children dancing and screaming over bonbons and toys that break, and shiny things that are of no use. Really, Mamma, I've had so many Christmases all alike that I don't think I can bear another one." And Effie laid herself flat on the sofa, as if the mere idea was too much for her.

Her mother laughed at her despair, but was sorry to see her little girl so discontented, when she had everything to make her happy, and had known but ten Christmas days.

"Suppose we don't give you any presents at all—how would that suit you?" asked Mamma, anxious to please her spoiled child.

"I should like one large and splendid one, and one dear little one, to remember some very nice person by," said Effie.

"Well, my darling, I will see what I can do to please you, and not say a word until all is ready. If I could only get a new idea to start with!" And Mamma went on tying up her pretty bundles with a thoughtful face, while Effie strolled to the window to watch the rain that kept her indoors and made her dismal.

"Seems to me poor children have better times than rich ones. I can't go out, and there is a girl about my age splashing along, without any maid to fuss about rubbers and cloaks and umbrellas and colds. I wish I was a beggar-girl."

"Would you like to be hungry, cold, and ragged, to beg all day, and sleep on an ash-heap at night?" asked Mamma. . . . "At the Orphan Asylum today I saw two dozen merry little souls who have no parents, no home, and no hope of Christmas beyond a stick of candy or a cake. I wish you had been there to see how happy they were, playing with the old toys some richer children had sent them."

You may give them all mine; I'm so tired of them I never want to see them again," said Effie.

"I will, and let you begin again with something you will not tire of, if I can only find it." And Mamma knit her brows trying to discover some grand surprise for this child who didn't care for Christmas. . . .

"I'll have a fairy tale tonight, a very interesting one," commanded Effie, as she put on her blue silk wrapper and little fur-lined slippers to sit before the fire and have her long curls brushed.

So Nursey told her best tales; and when at last the child lay down under her lace curtains, her head was full of a curious jumble of Christmas elves, poor children, snow-storms, sugar-plums, and surprises. So it is no wonder that she dreamed all night; and this was the dream, which she never quite forgot.

She found herself sitting on a stone, in the middle of a great field, all alone. The snow was falling fast, a bitter wind whistled by, and night was coming on. She felt hungry, cold, and tired, and did not know where to go nor what to do.

"I wanted to be a beggar-girl, and now I am one; but I don't like it, and wish somebody would come and take care of me. I don't know who I am, and I think I must be lost," thought Effie, with the curious interest one takes in one's self in dreams.

But the more she thought about it, the more bewildered she felt. Faster fell the snow, colder blew the wind, darker grew the night; and poor Effie made up her mind that she was quite forgotten and left to freeze alone. The tears were chilled on her cheeks, her feet

felt like icicles, and her heart died within her, so hungry, frightened, and forlorn was she. Laying her head on her knees, she gave herself up for lost, and sat there with the great flakes fast turning her to a little white mound, when suddenly the sound of music reached her, and starting up, she looked and listened with all her eyes and ears. . . .

A child's voice sang, a child's hand carried the little candle; and in the circle of soft light it shed, Effie saw a pretty child coming to her through the night and snow. A rosy, smiling creature, wrapped in white fur, with a wreath of green and scarlet holly on its shining hair, the magic candle in one hand, and the other outstretched as if to shower gifts and warmly press all other hands. . . .

"Dear child, you are lost, and I have come to find you," said the stranger, taking Effie's cold hands in his, with a smile like sunshine, while every holly berry glowed like a little fire.

"Do you know me?" asked Effie, feeling no fear, but a great gladness, at his coming.

"I know all children, and go to find them; for this is my holiday, and I gather them from all parts of the world to be merry with me once a year."

"Are you an angel?" asked Effie, looking for the wings.

"No; I am a Christmas spirit, and live with my mates in a pleasant place, getting ready for our holiday, when we are let out to roam about the world, helping to make this a happy time for all who will let us in. Will you come and see how we work?"

"I will go anywhere with you. Don't leave me again," cried Effie, gladly.

With a wave of his candle . . . the dismal field changed to a new world so full of wonders that all her troubles were forgotten in a minute.

Bells were ringing so merrily that it was hard to keep from dancing. Green gar-

A nineteenth-century Christmas card illustrates the decorations and toys of America in the 1800s. Photograph copyright Superstock.

lands hung on the walls, and every tree was a Christmas tree full of toys, and blazing with candles that never went out.

"That is so beautiful! I wish I could make merry Christmas as these good people do, and be loved and thanked as they are," said Effie, softly, as she watched the busy men and women do their work and steal away without thinking of any reward but their own satisfaction.

"You can if you will. I have shown you the way. Try it, and see how happy your own holiday will be hereafter."

As he spoke, the spirit seemed to put his arms about her, and vanished with a kiss.

"Darling, wake up, and tell me why you are smiling in your sleep," said a voice in her ear; and opening her eyes, there was Mamma bending over her, and morning sunshine streaming into the room. . . .

"The spirit said I could work lovely miracles if I tried; but I don't know how to begin, for I have no magic candle to make

feasts appear, and light up groves of Christmas trees, as he did," said Effie, sorrowfully.

"Yes, you have. We will do it! We will do it!" And clapping her hands, Mamma suddenly began to dance all over the room as if she had lost her wits.

"How? How? You must tell me, Mamma," cried Effie, dancing after her.

"No, no; it is a surprise—a grand surprise for Christmas day!" sung Mamma. "Now, come to breakfast; for we must work like bees if we want to play spirits tomorrow. You and Nursey will go out shopping, and get heaps of things, while I arrange matters behind the scenes."

They were running downstairs as Mamma spoke, and Effie called out breathlessly:

"It won't be a surprise; for I know you are going to ask some poor children here, and have a tree or something. It won't be like my dream; for they had ever so many trees, and more children than we can find anywhere."

"There will be no tree, no party, no dinner, in this house at all, and no presents for you. Won't that be a surprise?" And Mamma laughed at Effie's bewildered face.

"Do it. I shall like it, I think; and I won't ask any questions, so it will all burst upon me when the time comes," she said; and she ate her breakfast thoughtfully, for this really would be a new sort of Christmas.

All that morning Effie trotted after Nursey in and out of shops, buying dozens of barking dogs, wooly lambs, and squeaking birds; tiny tea-sets, gay picture-books, mittens and hoods, dolls and candy. Parcel after parcel was sent home; but when Effie returned she saw no trace of them, though she peeped everywhere. Nursey chuckled, but wouldn't give a hint, and went out again in the afternoon with a long list of more things to buy; while Effie wandered forlornly about the house, missing the usual merry stir that went before the Christmas dinner and the evening fun.

As for Mamma, she was quite invisible all day, and came in at night so tired that she could only lie on the sofa to rest, smiling as if some very pleasant thought made her happy in spite of weariness. . . .

Christmas morning was a very strange one; for when she woke there was no stocking to examine, no pile of gifts under her napkin, no one said, "Merry Christmas!" to her, and the dinner was just as usual to her. Mamma vanished again, and Nursey kept wiping her eyes and saying: "The dear things! It's the prettiest idea I ever heard of. No one but your blessed ma could have done it."

"Do stop, Nursey, or I shall go crazy because I don't know the secret!" cried Effie, more than once; and she kept her eye on the clock, for at seven in the evening the surprise was to come off.

The longed-for hour arrived at last, and the child was too excited to ask questions when Nursey put on her cloak and hood and led her to the carriage. They drove away, leaving their house the one dark and silent one in the row.

"I feel like the girls in the fairy tales who are led off to strange places and see fine things," said Effie, in a whisper, as they jingled through the gay streets.

"Ah, my deary, it *is* like a fairy tale, I do assure you, and you will see finer things than most children will tonight. . . ."

They drove into a dark yard, and Effie was led through a back door to a little room, where Nursey coolly proceeded to take off not only her cloak and hood but her dress and shoes also. Effie stared and bit her lips, but kept still until out of the box came a little white fur coat and boots, a wreath of holly leaves and berries, and a candle with a frill of gold paper round it. A long "Oh!" escaped her then; and when she was dressed and saw herself in the glass, she started back, exclaiming. "Why, Nursey, I look like the spirit in my dream!"

"So you do; and that's the part you are to play, my pretty! Now whist, while I blind your eyes and put you in your place."

"Shall I be afraid?" whispered Effie, full of wonder; for as they went out she heard the sound of many voices, the tramp of many feet, and, in spite of the bandage, was sure a great light shone upon her when she stopped.

"You needn't be; I shall stand close by, and your ma will be there."

After the handkerchief was tied about her eyes, Nursey led Effie up some steps, and placed her on a high platform, where something like leaves touched her head, and the soft snap of lamps seemed to fill the air.

Music began as soon as Nursey clapped her hands, the voices outside sounded nearer, and the tramp was evidently coming up the stairs.

"Now, my precious, look and see how you and your dear ma have made a merry Christmas for them that needed it!"

Off went the bandage; and for a minute Effie really did think she was asleep again, for she stood in "a grove of Christmas trees," all gay and shining as in her vision. Twelve on a side, in two rows down the room, stood the little pines, each on its low table; and behind Effie a taller one rose to the roof, hung with wreaths of popcorn, apples, oranges, horns of candy, and cakes of all sorts, from sugary hearts to gingerbread Jumbos. On the smaller trees she saw many of her own discarded toys and those Nursey bought, as well as heaps that seemed to have rained down straight from that delightful Christmas country where she felt as if she was again.

"How splendid! Who is it for? What is that noise? Where is Mamma?" cried Effie, pale with pleasure and surprise, as she stood looking down the brilliant little street from her high place.

Before Nursey could answer, the doors at the lower end flew open, and in marched twenty-four little blue-gowned orphan girls, singing sweetly, until amazement changed the song to cries of joy and wonder as the shining spectacle appeared. While they stood staring with round eyes at the wilderness of pretty things about them, Mamma stepped up beside Effie, and holding her hand fast to give her courage, told the story of the dream in a few simple words, ending in this way:

"So my little girl wanted to be a Christmas spirit too, and make this a happy day for those who had not as many pleasures and comforts as she has. She likes surprises, and we planned this for you all. She shall play the good fairy, and give each of you something from this tree, after which every

one will find her own name on a small tree, and can go to enjoy it in her own way. March by, my dears, and let us fill your hands."

Nobody told them to do it, but all the hands were clapped heartily before a single child stirred; then one by one they came to look up wonderingly at the pretty giver of the feast as she leaned down to offer them great yellow oranges, red apples, bunches of grapes, bonbons, and cakes, till all were gone, and a double row of smiling faces turned toward her as the children filed back to their places in the orderly way they had been taught.

Then each was led to her own tree by the good ladies who had helped Mamma with all their hearts. . . . How they ran to show one another the new treasures! How they peeped and tasted, pulled and pinched, until the air was full of queer noises, the floor covered with papers, and the little trees left bare of all but candles!

"I don't think heaven can be any better than this," sighed one small girl, as she looked about her in a blissful haze, holding her full apron with one hand, while she luxuriously carried sugar-plums to her mouth with the other.

"Is that a truly angel up there?" asked another, fascinated by the little white figure with the wreath on its shining hair, who in some mysterious way had been the cause of all this merry-making.

"I wish I dared to go and kiss her for this splendid party," said a lame child, leaning on her crutch as she stood near the steps, wondering how it seemed to sit in a mother's lap, as Effie was doing, while she watched the happy scene before her.

Effie heard her, and remembering Tiny Tim, ran down and put her arms about the pale child, kissing the wistful face, as she said sweetly, "You may; but Mamma deserves the thanks. She did it all; I only dreamed

A Christmas card, circa 1911, sends nostalgic greetings to all.
Photograph copyright Superstock.

about it."

Lame Katy felt as if "a truly angel" was embracing her, and could only stammer out her thanks, while the other children ran to see the pretty spirit, and touch her soft dress, until she stood in a crowd of blue gowns, laughing as they held up their gifts for her to see and admire.

Mamma leaned down and whispered one word to the older girls; and suddenly they all took hands to dance round Effie, singing as they skipped.

It was a pretty sight, and the ladies found it hard to break up the happy revel; but it was late for small people. . . . So the girls fell into line, and marched before Effie and Mamma again, to say good-night with such grateful little faces that the eyes of those who looked grew dim with tears. Mamma kissed every one; and many a hungry childish heart felt as if the touch of those tender lips was their best gift. Effie shook so many small hands that her own tingled; and when

Katy came she pressed a small doll into Effie's hand, whispering, "You didn't have a single present, and we had lots. Do keep that; it's the prettiest thing I got."

"I will," answered Effie, and held it fast until the last smiling face was gone, the surprise all over, and she safe in her own bed, too tired and happy for anything but sleep.

"Mamma, it *was* a beautiful surprise, and I thank you so much! I don't see how you ever did it; but I like it best of all the Christmases I ever had, and mean to make one every year. I had my splendid big present, and here is the dear little one to keep for love of poor Katy; so even that part of my wish came true."

And Effie fell asleep with a happy smile on her lips, her one humble gift still in her hand, and a new love for Christmas in her heart that never changed through a long life spent in doing good.

Christmas EVE

Mary Mapes Dodge

All night long the pine-trees wait,
Dark heads bowed in solemn state,
Wondering what may be the fate
    Of little Norway Spruce.

Little Norway Spruce who stood
Only lately in the wood.
Did they take him for his good—
    They who bore him off?

Little Norway Spruce so trim,
Lithe, and free, and strong of limb—
All the pines were proud of him!
    Now his place is bare!

All that night the little tree
In the dark stood patiently,
Far away from forest free,
    Laden for the morn.

Chained and laden, but intent,
On the pines his thoughts were bent;
They might tell him what it meant,
    If he could but go!

Morning came—the children. "See!
Oh, our glorious Christmas-tree!"
Gifts for everyone had he;
    Then he understood.

An exquisitely decorated Christmas tree brings memories of home.
Photograph copyright Steve Terrill.

A Child's PRAYER

Francis Thompson

Little Jesus, wast Thou shy
Once, and just as small as I?
And what did it feel like to be
Out of Heaven, and just like me?
Did'st Thou sometimes think of There,
And ask where all the angels were?
I should think that I would cry
For my house all made of sky;
I would look about the air,
And wonder where my angels were;
And at waking 'twould distress me—
Not an angel there to dress me!

Hadst Thou ever any toys,
Like us little girls and boys?
And didst Thou play in Heaven with all

The angels, that were not too tall,
With stars for marbles? Did the things
Play *Can you see me?* through their wings?
Didst Thou kneel at night to pray,
And didst Thou join Thy hands, this way?
And did they tire sometimes, being young,
And make the prayer seem very long?
And dost Thou like it best, that we
Should join our hands and pray to Thee?
I used to think, before I knew,
The prayer not said unless we do.

And did Thy Mother at the night
Kiss Thee and fold the clothes in right?
And didst Thou feel quite good in bed,
Kissed, and sweet, and Thy prayers said?
Thou canst not have forgotten all
That it feels like to be small;
And Thou knows't I cannot pray
To Thee in my father's way—
When Thou wast so little, say,
Could'st Thou talk in Thy Father's way?—
So, a little Child, come down
And hear a child's tongue like Thy own;
Take me by the hand and walk,
And listen to my baby talk,
To Thy Father show my prayer
(He will look, Thou art so fair),
And say: "O Father, I, Thy Son,
Bring the prayer of a little one."

And He will smile, that children's tongue
Hast not changed since Thou wast young!

A child's eyes convey all the wonder of Christmas and the miracle of the birth of Christ.
Painting by Frances Hook copyright Ideals Publications Incorporated.

Three STOCKINGS

Jan Struther

However much one groaned about it beforehand, however much one hated making arrangements and doing up parcels and ordering several days' meals in advance—when it actually happened, Christmas Day was always fun.

It began in the same way every year: the handle of her bedroom door being turned just loudly enough to wake her up, but softly enough not to count as waking her up on purpose; Toby glimmering like a moth in the dark doorway, clutching a nobbly Christmas stocking in one hand and holding up his pajama trousers with the other. (He insisted upon pajamas, but he had not yet outgrown his sleeping-suit figure.)

"Toby! It's only just after six. I did say not till seven."

"But, Mummy, I can't tell the time." He was barefoot and shivering, and his eyes were like stars.

"Come here and get warm, you little goat." He was into her bed in a flash, stocking and all. The tail of a clockwork dog scratched her shoulder. A few moments later another head appeared round the door, a little higher up.

"Judy, darling, it's too early, honestly."

"I know, but I heard Toby come in, so I knew you must be awake."

"All right, you can come into bed, but you've got to keep quiet for a bit. Daddy's still asleep."

And then a third head, higher up still, and Vin's voice, even deeper than it had been at Long Leave.

"I say, are the others in here? I thought I heard them."

He curled himself up on the foot of his father's bed. And by that time, of course, Clem was awake too. The old transparent stratagem had worked to perfection once more: there was nothing for it but to switch on the lights, shut the windows, and admit that Christmas Day had insidiously but definitely begun.

The three right hands—Vin's strong and broad, Judy's thin and flexible, Toby's still a star-fish—plunged in and out of the three distorted stockings, until there was nothing left but the time-hallowed tangerine in the toe. (It was curious how that tradition lingered, even nowadays when

A child decorating the family Christmas tree. Painting copyright Donald Zolan.

children had a good supply of fruit all the year round.) Their methods were as different as their hands. Vin, with little grunts of approval, examined each object carefully as he drew it out, exploring all its possibilities before he went on to the next. Judy, talking the whole time, pulled all her treasures out in a heap, took a quick glance at them and went straight for the one she liked best—a minikin baby in a wicker cradle. Toby pulled all his out, too, but he arranged them in a neat pattern on the eiderdown and looked at them for a long time in complete silence. Then he picked up one of them—a big glass marble with colored squirls inside—and put it by itself a little way off. After that he played with the other toys, appreciatively enough; but from time to time his eyes would stray towards the glass marble, as though to make sure it was still waiting for him.

Mrs. Miniver watched him with a mixture of delight and misgiving. It was her own favorite approach to life: but the trouble was that sometimes the marble rolled away. Judy's was safer; Vin's, on the whole, the wisest of the three.

To the banquet of real presents which was waiting downstairs, covered with a red and white dust-sheet, the stocking toys, of course, were only an *apéritif*; but they had a special and exciting quality of their own. Perhaps it was the atmosphere in which they were opened—the powerful charm of the miniature, of toy toys, of smallness squared; perhaps it was the sense of limitation within a strict form, which gives to both the filler and the emptier of a Christmas stocking something of the same enjoyment which is experienced by the writer and the reader of a sonnet; or perhaps it was merely that the spell of the old legend still persisted, even though for everybody in the room except

Toby the legend itself was outworn.

There were cross-currents of pleasure, too: smiling glances exchanged by her and Vin about the two younger children (she remembered suddenly, having been an eldest child, the unsurpassable sense of grandeur that such glances gave one); and by her and Clem, because they were both grown-ups; and by her and Judy, because they were both women; and by her and Toby, because they were both the kind that leaves the glass marble till the end. The room was laced with an invisible network of affectionate understanding.

This was one of the moments, thought Mrs. Miniver, which paid off at a

single stroke all the accumulations on the debit side of parenthood: the morning sickness and the quite astonishing pain; the pram in the passage, the cold mulish glint in the cook's eye; the holiday nurse who had been in the best families; the pungent white mice, the shrivelled caterpillars; the plasticine on the door-handles, the face-flannels in the bathroom, the nameless horrors down the crevices of armchairs; the alarms and emergencies, the swallowed button, the inexplicable earache, the ominous rash appearing on the eve of a journey; the school bills and the dentists' bills; the shortened step, the tempered pace, the emotional compro-

mises, the divided loyalties, the adventures continually forsworn.

And now Vin was eating his tangerine, pig by pig; Judy had undressed baby and was putting on its frock again back to front; Toby was turning the glass marble round and round against the light, trying to count the squirls. There were sounds of movement in the house; they were within measurable distance of the blessed chink of early morning tea. Mrs. Miniver looked towards the window. The dark sky had already paled a little in its frame of cherry-pink chintz. Eternity framed in domesticity. Never mind. One had to frame it in something, to see it at all.

Christmas MORNING

Phillips Brooks

The sky can still remember
The earliest Christmas morn,
When in the cold December
The Saviour Christ was born;
And still in darkness clouded,
And still in noonday light,
It feels its far depths crowded
With Angels fair and bright.

Shall we not listen while they sing,
This latest Christmas morn,
And music hear in everything,
And faithful lives in tribute bring
To the great song which greets the King
Who comes when Christ is born?

O never failing splendor!
O never silent song!
Still keep the green earth tender,
Still keep the gray earth strong;
Still keep the brave earth dreaming
Of deeds that shall be done,
While children's lives come streaming
Like sunbeams from the sun.

Pastel by Frances Hook suggests that children of today can still "go to the manger." Copyright Ideals Publications Incorporated.

Candlelit Heart

Mary E. Linton

Somewhere across the winter world tonight
You will be hearing chimes that fill the air;
Christmas extends its all-enfolding light
Across the distance . . . something we can share.

You will be singing, just the same as I,
These old familiar songs we know so well;
And you will see these same stars in your sky
And wish upon that brightest one that fell.

I shall remember you and trim my tree:
One shining star upon the topmost bough,
I will hang wreaths of faith that all may see.
Tonight I glimpse beyond the here and now.

And all the years that we must be apart
I keep a candle lighted in my heart.

A quaint New England village, covered with snow and decorated for Christmas, draws the whole community together as friends. Photograph copyright Johnson's Photography.

Christmas in a VILLAGE

John Clare

Each house is swept the day before,
And windows stuck with evergreens;
The snow is besomed from the door,
And comfort crowns the cottage scenes.
Gilt holly with its thorny pricks
And yew and box with berries small,
These deck the unused candlesticks,
And pictures hanging by the wall.

Neighbours resume their annual cheer,
Wishing with smiles and spirits high
Glad Christmas and a happy year
To every morning passer-by.
Milkmaids their Christmas journeys go
Accompanied with favoured swain,
And children pace the crumping snow
To taste their granny's cake again.

Hung with the ivy's veining bough,
The ash trees round the cottage farm
Are often stripped of branches now
The cottar's Christmas hearth to warm.
He swings and twists his hazel band,
And lops them off with sharpened hook,
And oft brings ivy in his hand
To decorate the chimney nook.

The shepherd now no more afraid,
Since custom doth the chance bestow,
Starts up to kiss the giggling maid
Beneath the branch of mistletoe
That 'neath each cottage beam is seen
With pearl-like berries shining gay,

The shadow still of what hath been
Which fashion yearly fades away.

And singers too, a merry throng,
At early morn with simple skill
Yet imitate the angel's song
And chant their Christmas ditty still;
And 'mid the storm that dies and swells
By fits—in hummings softly steals
The music of the village bells
Ringing round their merry peals.

And when it's past, a merry crew
Bedecked in masks and ribbons gay,
The morris dance their sports renew
And act their winter evening play.
The clown turned king for penny praise
Storms with the actor's strut and swell,
And harlequin to laugh to raise
Wears his hunchback and tinkling bell.

And oft for pence and spicy ale
With winter nosegays pinned before,
The wassail singer tells her tale
And drawls her Christmas carols o'er,
While prentice boy with ruddy face
And rime-bepowdered dancing locks
From door to door with happy pace
Runs round to claim his Christmas box.

*Christmas lights offer a glimpse of small-town holiday
warmth in Chelan County, Washington. Photograph
copyright Terry Donnelly.*

Christmas Eve in Our Village

Phyllis McGinley

Main Street is gay. Each lamppost glimmers,
        Crowned with a blue, electric star.
The gift tree by our fountain shimmers,
        Superbly tall, if angular
        (Donated by the Men's Bazaar).

With garlands proper to the times
        Our doors are wreathed, our lintels strewn.
From our two steeples sound the chimes,
        Incessant, through the afternoon,
        Only a little out of tune.

Breathless, with boxes hard to handle,
        The grocery drivers come and go.
Madam the Chairman lights a candle
        To introduce our club's tableau.
        The hopeful children pray for snow.

They cluster, mittened, in the park
        To talk of morning, half affrighted,
And early comes the winter dark
        And early are our windows lighted
        To beckon homeward the benighted.

The eggnog's lifted for libation,
        Silent at last the postman's ring,
But on the plaza near the station
        The carolers are caroling.
        "O Little Town!" the carolers sing.

A delightful and colorful village scene at Christmastime.
Painting by Jay Killian copyright Ideals Publications Incorporated.

In Praise of Christmas Letters

Marjorie Holmes

Deck the house with boughs of holly, 'tis the season to be jolly! I'm about to write our family Christmas letter: that glowing inventory of the year's events I've been saving up for the whole year. And as I pull the chair closer to my desk, it warms my heart to know that all over the country other people are as eagerly counting their blessings as they sit down to write theirs.

Never mind that Christmas letters have gotten bad press lately. "Brag sheets" they've been called. "Boring reports that nobody reads." Well, let the scoffers scoff, the Scrooges sneer. To me the annual exchange of these letters is one of the happiest customs to appear on the American scene. Not everyone writes them, but for those who do, they are a song of hope and joy in this troubled world, proclaiming that despite the trials that beset us all, each year of life is to be treasured. God is good!

Christmas letters also serve two useful purposes. First, they can forge a vital link between friends who don't want to lose each other. Second, your own letters, if you save them, will provide a record of life for your family, each one a small but shining chapter in its biography.

I began to write ours years ago. My husband had been transferred often by his company. In each city, wherever they sent him, there were always two or three couples who became especially dear to us. As we moved and the numbers grew, correspondence became impossible; we came to rely on notes scribbled once a year on Christmas cards. Finally I ran out of time and space even for notes, giving up one year in frustration after getting only as far as the M's on our list. It was either drop everybody, except for impersonal greetings, or find a better way.

Christmas letters were just getting started. We had received a few and were delighted, devouring every word. What a great idea. It might be fun as well as feasible to write our own.

Nothing has been more rewarding. Most of our friends began to respond in kind, and along the way new ones joined the parade, bubbling over with their news, until now it's a happy avalanche. Some of them are too long to read all at once, but they're always welcome, always savored, even if later, a few at a time. No matter that I don't know half the people they speak of, and can't hope to keep their children and grandchildren straight. What *matters* is that they haven't forgotten us. They are reaching out to us across the miles and the years, sharing their joys and their sorrows, believing that we still care enough about them to want to know.

To me this is life-enriching. I feel sorry for people who miss it. And I grieve for the loss of once-close friends who let all this slip away.

Among the Scrooges who would take the joy out of Christmas letters was a critic who wrote to Ann Landers, setting out rules for us eager innocents who write them. "Keep them short," he ordered. "Never more than a page. *Don't* describe your travels. And *never* send to people you don't know well."

Nuts! Cram the year's wonders onto a single page? You might as well tell Santa to travel light by dumping out half his toys. True, the shorter your letter the more likely it is to be read. But why spoil your own fun? And while you needn't make your Christmas letter a travelogue, we've done a lot of excellent armchair traveling with good friends. My husband and I save the longer, more colorful accounts to read aloud after the holidays. We've gone on African safaris with the Williamses, climbed the Alps with the Olsens, joined the Loschers on their visit to the Great Wall of China. We are thrilled for them and *with* them. There is vicarious pleasure in sharing their adventures, just as we feel they will take some small pleasure in sharing ours.

As for that edict about being very choosy about who gets your Christmas letters, nonsense! Let your heart prevail, along with your common sense. I have exchanged such letters with people from all walks of life, sometimes after a brief but somehow meaningful encounter, and occasionally with a reader or a writer I've never met.

Years after we moved away, the holidays were always brightened by a long newsy letter from the dear little Polish lady who used to sell us vegetables from her roadside stand. She loved us enough to know we'd always be interested—in the *kolacky* she was baking and boxing to send away to children now in college, the honors they were winning, the progress of her husband, war-crippled but always cheerful in his wheelchair. And as long as she lived, we responded in kind.

Every year I look forward to the letters of a Washington taxi driver who dropped me off at an autographing party one day and then dashed home to bring his wife. This man, Irving Schlaifer, has become a modest celebrity for his long Christmas letters detailing the small wonders of another year. Though he will give you a cab's-eye view of the state of the nation, and sometimes mention a notable just delivered to the White House, mainly it's the deal he got on a new car that's exciting—the sheen of its polish and the miles it gets to the gallon. It's celebrating another anniversary with Emma, the exact location of the beautiful restaurant where they dined, and the wonderful things on the menu. ("For dessert Emma chose cherries flambe. I decided on good old apple pie.") Frequently he includes the recipe for Emma's famous fruitcake, with this year's variations, and always, always, the names and antics of their family of cats.

Irving's letters are unique in their minutiae; few of us have time to write so much. But everybody on his long list adores them. Irving epitomizes the basic enthusiasm of the Christmas-letter writer, saying, in essence, "I'm proud of my job. I love my life and I love you. Here are my adventures. I hope you enjoy them. If not, I won't know the difference, but they've been fun for me!"

Adventures in living—that's what Christmas letters are all about. Most of them are joyful. I can't remember ever reading one that was filled with self-pity, doleful doings, or complaints. Not because we're being brave, or just reluctant to admit our failures, pain, and problems, but because at this season such things somehow dwindle in significance, lose their sting. Even the times when we must include important news such as divorce or a death in the family, these are related in terms of tenderness, faith, and hope for the bright new year.

No, at Christmas it isn't the burdens we long to express, it's the glow within us, the bounties and blessings. The achievements, the pleasures. And if some people are offended by reading of other people's happiness, in what they may consider "brag sheets," I'm not. I applaud. They are not meant to make me envious or affronted; they are paying me the compliment of believing that their news will be welcome. And as a friend I will rejoice.

But quite apart from other people's reactions to your Christmas letter, the truth is, you're not writing them for other people; *you are writing them for yourself.* You are harvesting these memories for the sheer joy of hugging them to your heart again, fixing them in time, setting them down. And if you keep them, they will be a rich harvest of memories for your family as well. Your Christmas letters can become their history. One-sided, yes, leaving out most of the troubles, but important in their statement that no matter what else may have happened during those difficult years, our life together was good.

I realized this recently when, in a box of old files, I found copies of some of our Christmas letters, many of them written long ago. Fascinated, I sat on the floor, reading all afternoon. . . .

The year I was rushed to the hospital the week before Christmas to deliver our baby girl (described in loving detail): "We brought her home on Christmas Eve. The kids had helped their dad trim an enormous tree in the window; its colored lights were

shining on the snow. Everybody gathered around, eyes sparkling as we unwrapped the precious bundle (her eyes were sparkling too, we're sure). But I'm afraid the boys were just as excited over the TV set Santa had brought early (our first) as they were over their new baby sister. . . ."

Again, "Mark, thirteen, is busting his buttons. His picture made the Washington *Evening Star* with his 100-pound marlin, the biggest caught so far this year. . . ."

Paper routes and Scouting, dancing lessons, cheerleading, the year Mickie was

prom queen, the graduations from high school or college. Moves, promotions, trips, remodeling a house, the thrill of a book or story sold.

On and on I read—events large or small, things I'd almost forgotten and which at the time probably meant little to anybody else. But oh, how important they were to us!

So many of those letters are missing. How I wish I had saved them all. But there are enough to gather together, every one I can find, and bind into booklets for my children. To refresh their memories, to read and laugh

Covered bridge over Pemigewasset River, New Hampshire. Photograph copyright Gene Ahrens.

about and cherish, perhaps to pass along.

That first Christmas, while the heavenly chorus sang, the angel proclaimed the birth of Jesus, saying, "I bring you good tidings of great joy, which shall be to all people!" Our Christmas letters are our hearts' carols proclaiming, "Joy to the world! We've made it through another year and life is good!"

Surely this is a beautiful thing.

A MERRY CHRISTMAS

now ...
Bethlehem ...
his thing which
... to pass; which
... hath made
... to us. 2.15

May your Christmas
be Joyous and Happy

JERUSALEM

Happy Christmas
Mild He lays His glory by
Born that man no more may die
Born to raise the sons of earth
Born to give them second birth.
C-47

hristmas
dismay,
was born to-day.

PEACE ON EARTH
GOOD WILL TO

Best
Christmas
Wishes

A hearty Christmas W

Lady Selecting Her Christmas Cards

Phyllis McGinley

Fastidiously, with gloved and careful fingers,
Through the marked samples she pursues her search.
Which shall it be: the snowscape's wintry languors
Complete with church,

An urban skyline, children sweetly pretty
Sledding downhill, the chaste, ubiquitous wreath,
Schooner or candle or the simple Scottie
With verse underneath?

Perhaps it might be better to emblazon
With words alone the stiff, punctilious square.
(Oh, not Victoria, certainly. This season
One meets it everywhere.)

She has a duty proper to the weather—
A Birth she must announce, a rumor to spread,
Wherefore the very spheres once sang together
And a star shone overhead.

Here are the Tidings which the shepherds panted
One to another, kneeling by their flocks.
And they will bear her name (engraved, not printed),
Twelve-fifty for the box.

A collection of antique Christmas cards, most dating from the nineteenth century.
Photograph copyright Jessie Walker Associates.

Six Green SINGERS

Eleanor Farjeon

The frost of the moon stood over my floor,
And six green singers stood at my door.

"What do ye here that music make?"
"Let us come in for Christ's sweet Sake."

"Long have ye journeyed in coming here?"
"Our Pilgrimage was the length of the year."

"Where do ye make for?" I asked of them.
"Our Shrine is a Stable in Bethlehem."

"What will ye do as ye go along?"
"Sing to the world an ever-green song."

"What will ye sing for the listening earth?"
"One will sing of a brave-souled Mirth,

"One of the Holiest Mystery,
The Glory of Glories shall one song be,

"One of the Memory of things,
One of the Child's imaginings,

"One of our songs is the fadeless Faith,
And all are of Life more mighty than death."

"Ere ye be gone that music make,
Give me an alms for Christ's sweet Sake."

"Six green branches we leave with you;
See they be scattered your house-place through.

"The staunch blithe Holly your board shall grace,
Mistletoe bless your chimney-place,

"Laurel to crown your lighted hall,
Over your bed let the Yew-bough fall,

"Close by the cradle the Christmas Fir,
For elfin dreams in its branches stir,

"Last and loveliest, high and low,
From ceil to floor let the Ivy go."

From each glad guest I received my gift
And then the latch of the door did lift—

"Green singers, God prosper the song ye make
As ye sing to the world for Christ's sweet Sake."

A magnificent cathedral is the backdrop for this group of carolers. Painting copyright Ideals Publications Incorporated.

Cherished and SHARED OF OLD

Susan Glaspell

"Thank goodness for the snow," thought Addie Morrison, as she watched the two children racing round the barn. And she was thinking it was nice there were some things that were everywhere—most everywhere: like sun and rain, like the wind and the snow, so's when you were sent far from your home there were these things—like the stars—to make you feel a little more at home in a distant land.

"Not a soul here they ever knew before," she would think of these two little Dutch children she'd taken into her home. They were warm now at night—not wandering on a road. They weren't hungry now— mercy no, she'd seen to *that,* but what are they *thinking,* she'd wonder, as at times they'd sit there so gravely. She wished they'd do more things they shouldn't, for when you're too good you must be a little afraid.

She hadn't been able to stand the pictures in the papers—so many tired children wanting to get back home. Her daughter Emmey, in the East, was working for little ones who had been turned out into the world. "Mother dear," she wrote, "I can't get home this Christmas—just can't. But I could send you two children for whom you could make a Christmas—the way you used to for me and Jack. You'll be so sorry for Johanna and Piet, and come to love them; perhaps you'll want them to stay on there with you in our old home. There were always children on the Morrison place."

So once more there were children on the old Morrison place, but could she make a happy Christmas for this little girl and boy bereft of their own? She could say "Merry Christmas," but could she make their hearts glad? And what is Christmas if there is not warmth within?

She didn't even know what they were used to for Christmas. She wished, for just five minutes, she could talk to their mother. "What would they like?" she'd ask. And their mother would reply—eagerly, so anxious: "Oh, if you would give them—" But this mother couldn't speak up for her children—struck down trying to hurry them to safety.

Germans did that. The Schultzes were Germans—over there in their fine house on the hill. And so her heart hardened anew against Emma Schultz—and that was good, for she found it not so easy to hate Emma at Christmas.

Never a Christmas they hadn't shared, all those years they were growing up. In this very kitchen they'd hung around sniffing and tasting. And when they weren't here they were at the Schultzes'. She had two homes—her own and the Schultzes'. And Emma had two—her own and the Morrisons'.

And then they had to act like that! Just to get a piece of land that didn't belong to them at all they'd fought John Morrison, best friend they'd had since they came—greenhorns—into this country. Country where the Morrisons had been since first there were white men in Iowa! Not to her dying day would she forget her father's face that late afternoon he came back from town, and standing by this very table said: "Well, they've won. The court has given them the strip. Don't ask me why. I don't know why. But I do know this! They've won the land—but they've lost the Morrisons. Never again—do you hear me, Addie?—never again can a Morrison be friend to a Schultz."

Memories were tricky things come Christmas-time. Maybe it was because you went on doing the same things. You made the cranberry sauce, trimmed the tree—doing alone the little things you'd done with the dearest friend you'd ever had.

For no one had ever taken Emma's place. Who could take the place of the friend with whom you'd shared all those good years of your life? Emma helped her make all her wedding things. Emma was there when her first baby was born. She'd named that daughter Emma. Later she'd thought of changing it—but not easy to change a name, and anyway she had an aunt named Emma—she got around it that way. And Walter. Emma was to have married Addie's brother Walter. But Walter went away to war—that other time the Germans tried to wreck the world—and he never came back. And they had comforted each other then.

Yes, laughter and sorrow they had

"Man's best friend," a friendly golden retriever, seeks shelter in the midst of a snowstorm. Photograph copyright Uniphoto.

shared. And how divided now! That fought-over land connected the Morrison and Schultz farms. Connected only to divide. It wasn't land—it was a gulf, a gulf that had widened with the years. . . . That is why there is hate in the world—(she half knew this, tried not to know)—hate unreasoning, living on because, one way or other, it got there in the first place; and when a thing has existed a long time it gives you the idea you can't change it—even makes you think you don't want to. . . .

"Come in and get warm!" she called to the children. "Stamp hard! Shake!" she cried gaily.

Well, if that little fellow wasn't edging up to the cookie jar. Good! You must think it's *your* house when you go after the cookie jar.

Johanna said, in her new careful English, "Thank you," for the cookie; little Piet

said something she didn't understand, but he smiled and she knew it was "Thank you."

What funny little cookies the Schultzes used to make for Christmas. Cut in all sorts of shapes—a rabbit, a star, a St. Nicholas and something called a grampus, and supposed to be for the bad child, but it had currants and nuts in it just the same, so who cared? Perhaps Johanna and Piet were used to cookies like that. Yes, Emma might know more than she did about what these children were used to. But Emma—warm in a fine sealskin coat—what did *she* care?

"Oh—pret-ty," she heard Johanna murmur, and turned to find her fingering a length of red ribbon that was to be tied on the tree.

Addie stood stock-still watching her, for the little girl's fingers moved over the bright stuff so wistfully, as if—as if she had once loved something like this.

"Time to dress ourselves up for Christmas," she said, slipping the bright broad ribbon under the collar of Johanna's sweater and making a fine red bow.

Then she began to laugh—Emma running after a pig, trying to catch the pig to tie a red ribbon round his neck. That was one of the crazy things they did together—dressing up the animals for Christmas. Well, Emma caught the pig, but fell down doing it and Emma and pig rolled over and over together—the pig squirming and Emma clutching. Addie could see them now and she went on laughing, until the children, thinking there must be something very funny indeed, politely joined in.

The snow continued to fall softly, knowing it was Christmas and the world should be white, and after the dinner things were cleared away, Addie wondered whether

A barn near Seager, New York, stands amid a snowstorm. Photograph copyright Gene Ahrens.

they'd like to be bundled up and go out again. That was the trouble—it was still hard to know for sure what they would like, for it wasn't *their* house yet.

But suddenly it was! What in the world were they looking at out that window—dancing up and down, catching hold of each other and squealing and pointing?

Oh, dear. Now what? For there he was—that miserable Schultz dog who came bounding over as if he didn't know a Schultz shouldn't come to the Morrisons'. She started for the door to go chase him away but the children thought she was going to let him in, and they were right upon her, all excited and happy—*natural*—for the first time they really were children. And all because that ugly Schultz dog—for some crazy reason called Doc—was standing there wagging his tail as if waiting for them to come out and play with him.

"We'll get a dog," she said. "A nice dog. This is the homeliest dog ever lived."

She tried to interest them in the dog they would have, but they wanted Doc and wanted him right now; and as Addie saw that first flare-up of joy begin to die down into disappointment, of course she couldn't stand it and there began a mad gay scramble to get them into their clothes so they could rush out and play with Doc Schultz.

Oh, they were so delighted! They could scarcely wait to get out—and then they were all in a scramble together, Doc jumping on them and waving his silly tail, and the children were laughing and screaming and they all went tearing away together.

And Addie Morrison sat there thinking it was strange—so very strange—that their first happy moment on the Morrison place came through Emma Schultz. . . .

Emma Schultz was remembering something herself. She was again a little girl not eight—new to America, a greenhorn.

And the children at school stared and laughed at her because she talked funny and didn't know their ways. But little Addie Morrison—so pretty then—came up and hooked her arm through Emma's and said: "You and me, let's us be friends."

More than anything else in the world she would like to walk over to Addie Morrison now, open the kitchen door just as she used to, and say—"You and me, let's us be friends."

At Christmas it was so hard not to remember. And this Christmas most of all, because again—after all these years—Addie was befriending the stranger. How good of Addie! How good of America! And she wondered if anyone could love America as did the one who had come here a stranger and been taken in.

She was the one to do something for these children, for who could know better than she what it was to be a child among things not familiar.

She was putting in a big jar the *Lebkuchen*, German Christmas cookies she made every year. She wouldn't have had the heart to make them this year, but her mother hadn't many Christmases left and clung to the things she was used to. . . .

Ten thousand times she'd wished that land in the bottom of the sea. What is land, compared to the love of friends? How gladly she would have given it back. . . . She'd like to cross that strip—and abolish it in crossing—open the kitchen door and see if there wasn't something she could do for these little children. But what nonsense. You couldn't change the way things were, and Addie had grown more bitter with the years. She'd shut the door—shut it in Emma Schultz's face.

"Emma! I hear Doc barking," her mother called out to her.

She opened her own kitchen door, and yes—there stood Doc. But—what in the world? He was all decorated for Christmas. A

red ribbon was wound round his collar and tied in a big gay bow. Now who could have done that?

And suddenly Emma Schultz sat down—so sure there was only one person in the world could have sent Doc home decorated for Christmas. Addie had not forgotten! Oh, she had sent a message saying she remembered. And Emma Schultz began hurrying fast as she could—getting the cookies, filling a big basket, hurrying into her boots, her coat, and out into the snow. She ran across the strip, giving it scarcely a thought, so eager to get to the Morrisons'.

But at the kitchen door she paused. So many years. . . . Then she knocked, and Addie opened the door.

"Why—why Emma Schultz," she said, as if she didn't know what to say.

"Merry Christmas, Addie," said Emma.

"Why—why—" And then all of a sudden Addie cried: "Merry Christmas yourself!"—and swiftly added: "For pity sakes come right in out of the snow!"

A little later they were all sitting round the kitchen stove, nibbling the cookies Emma had brought, Emma and Addie drinking tea and the children their cocoa—so cozy in the Morrison kitchen. . . .

"Emma!" Addie burst out with a laugh—"do you remember the *pig*?"

While they were laughing came a barking and scratching at the door and Johanna and Piet ran to let in their friend Doc.

As the children were busy brushing him off, Emma said, very low: "Oh, Addie— when he came home all fixed up for Christmas—and I knew you had remembered—were telling me you remembered—"

Addie had been sitting with her back to Doc. She turned now, and saw that the bow she had tied on Johanna at this moment adorned Emma's dog Doc.

And Emma thought she had done this! A Schultz thought a Morrison had made the first move. Ah, there was danger in that moment—danger the world has faced time and again. Old bitter loyalties—resentments of many years—right there, ready to rush in.

But something else came flooding into that moment: It was the children had done this. The children whom hate had driven here—brought love. How strange that this could be. Like a miracle it seemed.

She was afraid she was going to cry, so when Doc came sniffing up to the stove she said, almost crossly: "Why Emma Schultz— that dog's hungry.

"I'll tell you, children," she went on, "what do you say we give him our beef stew, for tomorrow we'll have turkey."

Doc knew it was to be for him and was dancing all around, his big bow bobbing. "Say Merry Christmas!" cried Addie, holding high the plate. Doc waved a hearty "Merry Christmas"—and they all watched Doc Schultz devour the Morrison stew.

The children clapped their hands at the speed with which he cleaned the plate. Emma and Addie smiled at each other—so much alive and warm between them. Dogs of other years were wearing their Christmas bows and cleaning the plate. In a changing world of many sorrows it can be sad to remember alone. But when friends share dear memories—a fire in the cold, light in the darkness.

And right there the children began a great clatter, running round in circles with Doc. Why, they weren't a *bit* afraid—for all the world as if they knew something had happened there amongst them. Whether they knew it or not, it was true—how blessed and true—that fear flew out through the window when love came in the door.

Blessings of ANGELS

Christmas Hymn

Richard Watson Gilder

Tell me what is this innumerable throng
Singing in the heavens a loud angelic song?
These are they who come with swift and shining feet
From round about the throne of God the Lord of Light to greet.

O who are these that hasten beneath the starry sky,
As if with joyful tidings that through the world shall fly?
The faithful shepherds these, who greatly were afeared
When, as they watched their flocks by night, the heavenly
    host appeared.

Who are these that follow across the hills of night
A star that westward hurries along the fields of light?
Three wise men from the east who myrrh and treasure bring
To lay them at the feet of him their Lord and Christ and King.

What babe new-born is this that in a manger cries?
Near on her bed of pain his happy mother lies?
O see! the air is shaken with white and heavenly wings—
This is the Lord of all the earth, this is the King of Kings.

Tell me, how may I join in this holy feast
With all the kneeling world, and I of all the least?
Fear not, O faithful heart, but bring what most is meet:
Bring love alone, true love alone, and lay it at his feet.

The angels making music, a detail from THE ANNUNCIATION TO THE SHEPHERDS, painted
by a sixteenth-century artist. Photograph copyright Christie's Images/Superstock.

The Smallest ANGEL

Elsie Binns

The smallest angel saw them go—
Stepping, dignified and slow
Down the shining golden stair,
Through the frosty midnight air.

"Fear not! fear not! To you we bring
Tidings of a new-born King."
Cherubim and seraphim
Chanted thus their Christmas hymn.

The smallest angel saw them go—
Stepping, dignified and slow.
Then, down the shining banister
He slid with tiny wings a-whir

Down to where the Baby lay
Snug and warm in fragrant hay.
"Fear not!" he whispered, "little King,
You are the tidings that they bring!"

A small angel playing a lute; painting by sixteenth-century Rosso Fiorentino, now in the Galleria Deglia Uffizi, Florence, Italy. Photograph copyright Superstock.

Heaven Cannot HOLD HIM

Christina Rossetti

Our God, heaven cannot hold him,
     Nor earth sustain;
Heaven and earth shall flee away
     When he comes to reign:
In the bleak mid-winter
     A stable-place sufficed
The Lord God Almighty
     Jesus Christ.

Enough for him whom cherubim
     Worship night and day,
A breastful of milk
     And a mangerful of hay;
Enough for him whom angels
     Fall down before,
The ox and ass and camel
     Which adore.

Angels and archangels
     May have gathered there,
Cherubim and seraphim
     Thronged the air,
But only his mother
     In her maiden bliss
Worshipped the Beloved
     With a kiss.

What can I give Him,
     Poor as I am?
If I were a shepherd
     I would bring a lamb,
If I were a Wise Man,
     I would do my part,
Yet what I can give Him?
     Give my heart.

The First Noel

Old English Carol

W. Sandys

1. The first No - el the an - gel did say, Was to cer - tain poor
2. They look - ed up and saw a star Shin-ing in the
3. And by the light of that same star The wise men
4. Then let us all with one ac - cord Sing prais - es

shep-herds in fields as they lay; In fields where they lay
east, be - yond them far, And to the earth it
came from coun - try far; To seek for a king was
to our heav - en - ly Lord Who hath made heav'n and

keep-ing their sheep, On a cold win-ter's night that was so deep.
gave great light, And so it con - tin - ued both day and night.
their in - tent, And to fol - low the star wher - ev - er it went. No -
earth of naught, And with His blood man - kind hath bought.

el, No - el, No - el, No - el, Born is the King of Is - ra - el.

Angels We Have Heard on High

Angels from the REALMS OF GLORY

James Montgomery

Henry Smart

1. An - gels, from the realms of glo - ry, Wing your flight o'er
2. Shep - herds, in the fields a - bid - ing, Watch - ing o'er your
3. Sag - es, leave your con - tem - pla - tions, Bright - er vi - sions
4. Saints, be - fore the al - tar bend - ing, Watch - ing long in

all the earth; Ye who sang cre - a - tion's sto - ry,
flocks by night, God with man is now re - sid - ing,
beam a - far; Seek the great De - sire of na - tions,
hope and fear, Sud - den - ly the Lord, de - scend - ing,

Now pro - claim Mes - si - ah's birth: Come and wor - ship,
Yon - der shines the in - fant Light: Come and wor - ship,
Ye have seen the In - fant's star: Come and wor - ship,
In His tem - ple shall ap - pear: Come and wor - ship,

come and wor - ship, Wor - ship Christ, the new - born King!
come and wor - ship, Wor - ship Christ, the new - born King!
come and wor - ship, Wor - ship Christ, the new - born King!
come and wor - ship, Wor - ship Christ, the new - born King!

There's a Song
IN THE AIR

Josiah G. Holland

B.F. White

1. There's a song in the air! There's a star in the sky! There's a
2. There's a tu - mult of joy O'er the won - der - ful birth, For the
3. In the light of that star Lie the a - ges im - pearled, And that
4. We re - joice in the light, And we ech - o the song That comes

moth - er's deep prayer And a ba - by's low cry! And the
Vir - gin's sweet Boy Is the Lord of the earth. Ay! the
song from a - far Has swept o - ver the world. Ev - 'ry
down thru the night From the heav - en - ly throng. Ay! we

star rains its fire while the beau - ti - ful sing, For the
star rains its fire while the beau - ti - ful sing, For the
hearth is a - flame and the beau - ti - ful sing In the
shout to the love - ly e - van - gel they bring, And we

man - ger of Beth - le - hem cra - dles a King!
man - ger of Beth - le - hem cra - dles a King!
homes of the na - tions that Je - sus is King!
greet in His cra - dle our Sav - ior and King!

It Came Upon the Midnight Clear

Edmund H. Sears

Richard S. Willis

1. It came up-on the mid-night clear, That glo-rious song of old, From
2. Still thro' the clo-ven skies they come, With peace-ful wings un-furled, And
3. All ye, be-neath life's crush-ing load, Whose forms are bend-ing low, Who
4. For lo! the days are has-t'ning on, By proph-et bards fore-told, When

an - gels bend - ing near the earth, To touch their harps of gold: "Peace
still their heaven - ly mu - sic floats O'er all the wea - ry world; A -
toil a - long the climb - ing way With pain - ful steps and slow, Look
with the ev - er - cir - cling years Comes round the age of gold; When

on the earth, good will to men," From heav'n's all - gra - cious King. The
bove its sad and low - ly plains They bend on hov - er-ing wing, And
now! for glad and gold - en hours Come swift - ly on the wing: O
peace shall o - ver all the earth Its an - cient splen - dors fling, And

world in sol - emn still - ness lay, To hear the an - gels sing.
ev - er o'er its Ba - bel sounds The bless-ed an - gels sing!
rest be - side the wea - ry road, And hear the an - gels sing!
the whole world give back the song Which now the an - gels sing.

Hark! The Herald Angels Sing

Christmas Song

Bliss Carman

Above the weary waiting world,
Asleep in chill despair,
There breaks a sound of joyous bells
Upon the frosted air.
And o'er the humblest rooftree, lo,
A star is dancing on the snow.

What makes the yellow star to dance
Upon the brink of night?
What makes the breaking dawn to glow
So magically bright,
And all the earth to be renewed
With infinite beatitude?

The singing bells, the throbbing star,
The sunbeams on the snow,
And the awakening heart that leaps,
New ecstasy to know,
They all are dancing in the morn
Because a little child is born.

Window in Carlisle Cathedral, Carlisle, England. Photograph
copyright The Crosiers, Gene Plaisted, OSC.

The Miraculous
Staircase

Arthur Gordon

On that cool December morning in 1878, sunlight lay like an amber rug across the dusty streets and adobe houses of Santa Fe. It glinted on the bright tile roof of the almost completed Chapel of Our Lady of Light and on the nearby windows of the convent school run by the Sisters of Loretto. Inside the convent, the Mother Superior looked up from her packing as a tap came on her door.

"It's another carpenter, Reverend Mother," said Sister Francis Louise, her round face apologetic. "I told him that you're leaving right away, that you haven't time to see him, but he says. . . ."

"I know what he says," Mother Magdalene said, going on resolutely with her packing. "That he's heard about our problem with the new chapel. That he's the best carpenter in all of New Mexico. That he can build us a staircase to the choir loft despite the fact that the brilliant architect in Paris who drew the plans failed to leave any space for one. And despite the fact that five master carpenters have already tried and failed. You're quite right, Sister; I don't have time to listen to that story again."

"But he seems such a nice man," said Sister Francis Louise wistfully, "and he's out there with his burro, and. . . ."

"I'm sure," said Mother Magdalene with a smile, "that he's a charming man, and that his burro is a charming donkey. But there's sickness down at the Santo Domingo pueblo, and it may be cholera. Sister Mary Helen and I are the only ones here who've had cholera. So we have to go. And you have to stay and run the school. And that's that!" Then she called, "Manuela!"

A young Indian girl of 12 or 13, black-haired and smiling, came in quietly on moccasined feet. She was a mute. She could hear and understand, but the Sisters had been unable to teach her to speak. The Mother Superior spoke to her gently: "Take my things down to the wagon, child. I'll be right there." And to Sister Francis Louise: "You'd better tell your carpenter friend to come back in two or three weeks. I'll see him then."

"Two or three weeks! Surely you'll be home for Christmas?"

"If it's the Lord's will, Sister. I hope so."

In the street, beyond the waiting wagon, Mother Magdalene could see the carpenter, a bearded man, strongly built and taller than most Mexicans, with dark eyes and a smiling, wind-burned face. Beside him, laden with tools and scraps of lumber, a small gray burro stood patiently. Manuela was stroking its nose, glancing shyly at its owner. "You'd better explain," said the Mother Superior, "that the child can hear him, but she can't speak."

Goodbyes were quick—the best kind when you leave a place you love. Southwest, then, along the dusty trail, the mountains purple with shadow, the Rio Grande a ribbon of green far off to the right. The pace was slow, but Mother Magdalene and Sister Mary Helen amused themselves by singing songs and telling Christmas stories as the sun marched up and down the sky. And their leathery driver listened and nodded.

Two days of this brought them to Santo Domingo Pueblo, where the sickness was not cholera after all, but measles, almost as deadly in an Indian village. And so they stayed, helping the harassed Father Sebastian, visiting the dark adobe hovels where feverish brown children tossed and fierce Indian dogs showed their teeth.

At night they were bone-weary, but sometimes Mother Magdalene found time to talk to Father Sebastian about her plans for the dedication of the new chapel. It was to be in April; the Archbishop himself would be there. And it might have been dedicated sooner, were it not for this incredible business of a choir loft with no means of access—unless it were a ladder.

"I told the Bishop," said Mother Magdalene, "that it would be a mistake to have the plans drawn in Paris. If something went wrong, what could we do? But he wanted our chapel in Santa Fe patterned after the Sainte Chapelle in Paris, and who am I to argue with Bishop Lamy? So the talented Monsieur Mouly designs a beautiful choir loft high up under the rose window, and no way to get to it."

"Perhaps," sighed Father Sebastian,

The Virgin and Child window in Ripon Cathedral, Ripon, England. Photograph copyright The Crosiers, Gene Plaisted, OSC.

"he had in mind a heavenly choir. The kind with wings."

"It's not funny," said Mother Magdalene a bit sharply. "I've prayed and prayed, but apparently there's no solution at all. There just isn't room on the chapel floor for the supports such a staircase needs."

The days passed, and with each passing day Christmas drew closer. Twice, horsemen on their way from Santa Fe to Albuquerque brought letters from Sister Francis Louise. All was well at the convent, but Mother Magdalene frowned over certain paragraphs. "The children are getting ready for Christmas," Sister Francis Louise wrote in her first letter. "Our little Manuela and the carpenter have become great friends. It's amazing how much he seems to know about us all. . . ."

And what, thought Mother Magdalene, is the carpenter still doing there?

The second letter also mentioned the carpenter. "Early every morning he comes

with another load of lumber, and every night he goes away. When we ask him by what authority he does these things, he smiles and says nothing. We have tried to pay him for his work, but he will accept no pay. . . ."

Work? What work? Mother Magdalene wrinkled up her nose in exasperation. Had that soft-hearted Sister Francis Louise given the man permission to putter around in the new chapel? With firm and disapproving hand, the Mother Superior wrote a note ordering an end to all such unauthorized activities. She gave it to an Indian pottery-maker on his way to Santa Fe.

But that night the first snow fell, so thick and heavy that the Indian turned back. Next day at noon the sun shone again on a world glittering with diamonds. But Mother Magdalene knew that another snowfall might make it impossible for her to be home for Christmas. By now the sickness at Santo Domingo was subsiding. And so that afternoon they began the long ride back.

The snow did come again, making their slow progress even slower. It was late on Christmas Eve, close to midnight, when the tired horses plodded up to the convent door. But lamps still burned. Manuela flew down the steps, Sister Francis Louise close behind her. And chilled and weary though she was, Mother Magdalene sensed instantly an excitement, an electricity in the air that she could not understand.

Nor did she understand it when they led her, still in her heavy wraps, down the corridor, into the new, as-yet-unused chapel where a few candles burned. "Look, Reverend Mother," breathed Sister Francis Louise. "Look!"

Like a curl of smoke the staircase rose before them, as insubstantial as a dream. Its top rested against the choir loft. Nothing else supported it; it seemed to float on air. There were no banisters. Two complete spirals it made, the polished wood gleaming softly in the candlelight. "Thirty-three steps," whispered Sister Francis Louise. "One for each year in the life of Our Lord."

Mother Magdalene moved forward like a woman in a trance. She put her foot on the first step, then the second, then the third. There was not a tremor. She looked down, bewildered, at Manuela's ecstatic, upturned face. "But it's impossible! There wasn't time!"

"He finished yesterday," the Sister said. "He didn't come today. No one has seen him anywhere in Santa Fe. He's gone."

"But who was he? Don't you even know his name?"

The sister shook her head, but now Manuela pushed forward, nodding emphatically. Her mouth opened; she took a deep, shuddering breath; she made a sound that was like a gasp in the stillness. The nuns stared at her, transfixed. She tried again. This time it was a syllable, followed by another. "Jo-sé." She clutched the Mother Superior's arm and repeated the first word she had ever spoken. "José!"

Sister Francis Louise crossed herself. Mother Magdalene felt her heart contract. José—the Spanish word for Joseph. Joseph the Carpenter. Joseph the Master Woodworker of. . . .

"José!" Manuela's dark eyes were full of tears. "José!"

Silence, then, in the shadowy chapel. No one moved. Far away across the snow-silvered town Mother Magdalene heard a bell tolling midnight. She came down the stairs and took Manuela's hand. She felt uplifted by a great surge of wonder and gratitude and compassion and love. And she knew what it was. It was the spirit of Christmas. And it was upon them all.

Angels, a detail from JOURNEY OF THE MAGI on the wall of the apse of the Palazzo Medici-Riccardi, Florence, Italy. Painted by Benozzo Gozzoli. Photograph copyright Superstock.

Blessings of SHEPHERDS

A Cradle Song

Padraic Colum

O men from the fields!
Come gently within.
Tread softly, softly,
O! men coming in.

Mavourneen is going
From me and from you,
Where Mary will fold him
With mantle of blue!

From reek of the smoke
And cold of the floor,
And the peering of things
Across the half-door.

O men from the fields!
Soft, softly come through—
Mary puts round him
Her mantle of blue.

*Painting by an unknown artist captures
the isolation of the shepherds and the
magnificent sight of the star. Painting
copyright Ideals Publications Incorporated.*

Outlanders, Whence Come Ye Last?

William Morris

Outlanders, whence come ye last?
   The snow in the street and the wind on the door.
Through what green seas and great have ye passed?
   Minstrels and maids, stand forth on the floor.

O ye shepherds, what have ye seen,
   The snow in the street and the wind on the door.
To slay your sorrow and heal your teen?
   Minstrels and maids, stand forth on the floor.

In an ox-stall this night we saw,
   The snow in the street and the wind on the door.
A Babe and a maid without a flaw.
   Minstrels and maids, stand forth on the floor.

There was an old man there beside,
   The snow in the street and the wind on the door.
His hair was white and his hood was wide.
   Minstrels and maids, stand forth on the floor.

And as we gazed this thing upon,
   The snow in the street and the wind on the door.
Those twain knelt down to the Little One.
   Minstrels and maids, stand forth on the floor.

And a marvelous song we straight did hear,
   The snow in the street and the wind on the door.
That slew our sorrow and healed our care.
   Minstrels and maids, stand forth on the floor.

News of a fair and a marvelous thing,
   The snow in the street and the wind on the door.
Nowell, nowell, nowell, we sing!
   Minstrels and maids, stand forth on the floor.

A magnificent sunrise over Afton, Virginia. Photograph copyright Superstock.

While Shepherds Watched
Their Flocks by Night

Margaret Deland

Like small curled feathers, white and soft,
    The little clouds went by,
Across the moon, and past the stars,
    And down the western sky;
In upland pastures, where the grass
    With frosted dew was white,
Like snowy clouds the young sheep lay,
    That first, best Christmas night.

The shepherds slept, and, glimmering faint,
    With twist of thin, blue smoke,
Only their fire's crackling flames
    The tender silence broke—
Save when a young lamb raised his head,
    Or when the night wind blew,
A nesting bird would softly stir,
    Where dusky olives grew—

With finger on her solemn lip,
    Night hushed the shadowy earth,
And only stars and angels saw
    The little Saviour's birth;
Then came such flash of sliver light
    Across the bending skies,
The wondering shepherds woke and hid
    Their frightened, dazzled eyes!

And all their gentle sleepy flock
    Looked up, then slept again,
Nor knew the light that dimmed the stars
    Brought endless Peace to men—
Nor even heard the gracious words
    That down the ages ring—
"The Christ is born! the Lord has come,
    Good-will on earth to bring!"

Then o'er the moonlit, misty fields,
    Dumb with the world's great joy,
The shepherds sought the white-walled town,
    Where lay the baby boy—

And oh, the gladness of the world,
    The glory of the skies,
Because the longed-for Christ looked up
    In Mary's happy eyes!

Painting by John Walter captures the shock of the shepherds in the star's bright light. Painting copyright Ideals Publications Incorporated.

The Little Christmas DONKEY

Geraldine Farrar

Great Herod on his golden throne
    Did in his wrath and fear
Decree that every tiny babe
    Should perish far and near.

Sweet Mary's gentle heart stood still,
    Oppressed by such a plight;
But God's bright angel came to her
    And counselled secret flight.

The little donkey stood close by.
    His soft eyes seemed to say:
"O trust in me, and have no fear,
    For I will lead the way."

Then gently on his furry back,
    Was cradled Mary sweet;
And so she rode to music
    Of the little donkey's feet.

He plodded o'er the desert sand,
    And bravely made his way,
Until before an inn they stopped,
    To ask if they might stay.

Alas, the inn was crowded full!
    There was no room at all,
Save in the lowly stable there,
    Beside the oxen stall.

Sweet Mary sank upon the straw,
    And lo! a wondrous sight!
For as the Holy Child was born,
    The world grew dazzling bright.

The splendid wings of angels
    Did brush the sleeping earth,
Their joyous carols telling
    The news of Jesus' birth.

One shining star shone out above,
    And in its silver ray,
The little donkey also kneeled
    On this first Christmas day.

And there he lay beside the Child;
    His feet were sore and worn;
Yet never counted he the pain,
    The burden he had borne.

His was a true if humble way
    To give his very best.
He did his nearest duty,
    And to God left all the rest.

So, little children, when you see him,
    Patient, with good will,
Remember how he served our Lord,
    And *never* use him ill.

The Song of a Shepherd Boy AT BETHLEHEM

Josephine Preston Peabody

Sleep, Thou little Child of Mary:
Rest Thee now.
Though these hands be rough from shearing
And the plough,
Yet they shall not ever fail Thee,
When the waiting nations hail Thee,
Bringing palms unto their King.
Now—I sing.

Sleep, Thou little Child of Mary,
Hope divine,
If Thou wilt but smile upon me,
I will twine
Blossoms for Thy garlanding.
Thou'rt so little to be King,
God's Desire!
Not a brier
Shall be left to grieve Thy brow;
Rest Thee now.

Sleep, Thou little Child of Mary.
Some fair day
Wilt Thou, as Thou wert a brother,
Come away
Over hills and over hollow?
All the lamps will up and follow,
Follow but for love of Thee.
Lov'st Thou me?

Sleep, Thou little Child of Mary;
Rest Thee now.

I that watch am come from sheep-stead
And from plough.
Thou wilt have disdain of me
When Thou'rt lifted, royally,
Very high for all to see:
Smilest Thou?

Painting by an unknown artist depicts the humble setting of the birth of Jesus.
Painting copyright Ideals Publications Incorporated.

The Glory of
THE GRASS

Claire Wallace Flynn

In what far Judean field
Did these upgrowing grasses yield
Their promises of gentle strength
When they should cradle Him at length?

What secret grace did earth produce,
That made those grasses for His use?
What glory from the sun they drew,
And what of pity from the dew?

What lad with sudden singing heart,
From all the other lads apart,
Cut them and bound them in the sun
And went his way—his work all done?

What tender girl, dark-haired and brown,
Carried the sheaves into the town;
Nor felt the weight of all that load
Along the narrow, hilly road?

And then the night, when Mary's face
Grew pallid in that lowly place,
Who filled the manger, made the bed,
Where only dumb beasts long had fed?

The humblest thing that grows on earth,
You gave Him comfort at His birth,
And kept Him warm, and made a nest,
Wherein His tiny limbs might rest!

Still with strange blindness have we trod
Amongst the common fields of God,
Seeing but dimly as we pass
The ancient glory of the grass!

*The shepherds and the angels, a stained glass window in Resurrection Church,
Eveleth, Minnesota. Photograph copyright The Crosiers, Gene Plaisted, OSC.*

The Stable of
THE INN

Thomas Nelson Page

It was in the twenty-seventh year of the reign of Augustus Caesar, or, as some say, in quite another year—in what was known simply as the tenth month, or, by another account, at the beginning of the eighth month. Toward the eventide of a calm day, two travellers of the peasant class, a man and a young woman—the latter riding an ass, beside which the man walked—toiled slowly up the rough highway that climbed the rocky hills a little to the southward of the ancient capital of Judea where Herod now reigned. . . . The wayfarers had journeyed all day, and the woman was faint with fatigue. At length she spoke to the man. He bowed his head and, as they reached a convenient point, turned out of the rough and dusty highway, and at a little distance came to a halt in a sloping, bare field to one side, in which, on an outjut of rock, stood an old and rude tower, lifted above the folds along a ledge of the hill—the tower of Eder. On the lower hills beyond the far edge of the field some shepherds were minding their flocks as they grazed their way slowly homeward along the sides of the rocky ravines which seamed the range.

Moving far enough into the field to be beyond the dust and noise of the highway, and, if necessary, to seek refuge in the tower, the man helped the woman to dismount with more gentleness than was usually shown by people of their class.

The man was already past middle age and, though of the peasant class, his face was strong and his features good, like so many of his race. The woman, young enough to be his daughter, might have been taken for his wife, save for a certain distance in his manner toward her. Having helped her down, he spoke softly and spread his robe on the ground for her to sit upon.

From a little distance floated upward the bleating of sheep, and presently the flocks began to appear, winding up from the lower slopes, led by their shepherds toward the folds built on the sides of the hills. To the woman's sigh of fatigue the man replied soothingly that they would soon be at their journey's end—at Bethlehem.

"Little Bethlehem!" murmured the young woman.

"'And thou Bethlehem, in the land of Juda, art not the least among

Painting by Grinnel showing Mary with the Baby Jesus and Joseph walking, as the family leaves the town of Bethlehem. Painting copyright Ideals Publications Incorporated.

the princes of Juda,'" quoted the man. "'For out of thee shall come a governor that shall rule my people Israel.' But thou art faint. The bottle is dry. The child that cried to us for water took the last drop. I will try to get thee some. The shepherds yonder will have it." She said something of her fear for him if he went among strange men, for the road from Jericho, which they had lately crossed, was infested with robbers—and the shepherds were a wild and reckless class. He reassured her and left her. . . . When he returned a little later, he bore in his hand a bottle of milk and a piece of the coarse bread that the shepherds eat. Not long afterward the shepherds themselves came over, one after one; plain; bearded; beaten by the weather; tanned by the sun; men of the field, with their stout staves, their sheepskin coats and goat-skin leggings, and their bags, or scrips, hung over their shoulders. At their approach the young woman, who was soon to be a mother, shyly drew about her her veil, which was ample enough to cover her from head to foot. The man as quietly moved forward and, interposing between her and the strangers, greeted the leader. But they were friendly. They wanted to talk.

"Thou art from Galilee?" queried the shepherd in the lead, a rough, grizzled man with eyes that burned deep under his shaggy brows. "Thy speech is Galilean?"

The other man bowed.

"Of Nazareth."

"Thy name is—what?"

"Joseph, son of Jacob."

"Dost thou look for the coming one?"

Joseph bowed.

"Whither goest thou?" asked the shepherd. "Jerusalem is behind thee."

"To Bethlehem, to meet the tax and be enrolled."

"Ah! The tax! The tax! It is always the tax," exclaimed the shepherd, while the oth-

ers growled their assent. "Why should they enroll us! To slay us? Did not King David try it! And how many men did it cost! Would that we had more like Judas! Art thou of Bethlehem?" he added.

"Yea, of the tribe and lineage of David. Both of us."

He glanced around to where the young woman sat.

The speech evidently made a further impression on the shepherds.

The young woman rose from the ground and Joseph lifted her gently to her saddle.

"Have a care of thy wife," said the shepherd. "She is young and the soldiers—"

"I have no fear," said Joseph calmly.

"They fear not God, nor regard man. To them an Israelite is a dog."

"We have no fear," said Joseph firmly.

"The place will be full. There is but one inn, and it will be crowded. They have been passing since sunrise. Clouds of dust on the road all day. We could see it from the hills."

The others assented.

"God will provide for us," said Joseph, as, bidding the shepherd adieu, he turned the ass's head toward the road.

The shepherds stood and watched them as they moved slowly upward until they were lost in the shadows on the highway, and then turned back to their flocks.

For nearly two hours the travellers plodded onward up the mountain. The village on its shoulder above them turned pink, then white as alabaster; and then the white faded to an icy blue; once more flushed to a saffron hue, and gradually died until by the time the travellers reached the nearest houses down the slope all was dusk, and with the darkness had come the cold. Once they paused at a turn in the road, and rested while they gazed across the dark valley to the eastward, to where some miles away gleamed many lights. "There it is," said Joseph. "There is Jerusalem. The Temple."

When they arrived at the village itself, they found what the shepherds had said to be true. The village was quite full and the only inn there had no place for them.

When they reached the gateway of the entrance court, travellers were being turned away, and a number of them were consulting together as to whether they should remain in the street all night or should go back toward Jerusalem. The gates would be shut; but they might find a lodging place in some other village.

It was dark, for the moon, though nearly full, was not yet risen above the hills, and it was too late to seek shelter elsewhere. Joseph went boldly to the gate and knocked. For some time there was no answer; but he continued to knock. Jeers broke out from the group in the street behind him; but he paid no heed. He kept on knocking. After a while the bar was drawn on the inside, and the porter partly opened the gate. When, however, he saw only a plain man with a woman mounted on an ass, he spoke shortly and told him that there was no room for them in the inn. Joseph made known his situation. His wife could go no farther and could not remain in the street all night. This did not avail. The porter spoke with contempt. "Better than you have been turned away tonight."

"Than me?—Yes," said Joseph; "but not better than that I bring." He took from his scrip an official paper and added that he had come "under Caesar's order."

"You trouble me much," growled the porter. But he admitted them, and told Joseph that he might spend the night in the stable if he could find a place there.

"In the stable!" said Joseph.

"Yes, and you'd better be glad to get that," growled the porter.

Joseph said that he was glad to have

the stable, and, leading the ass inside the gate, he followed the direction of the porter. He picked his way carefully across the dim court, amid the camels and asses crowded therein, and crossed over to the side to which the porter carelessly waved him, where, hollowed in the rock, were the rough caves used as stables for the inn.

Here in a stall which had, perhaps, been kept vacant in the hope that some guest of quality might come who would pay for it, and would bring honor to the inn, Joseph placed his wife, using such means as he could to make her comfortable.

The inn itself was full of life and movement; lights flared and failed and flared again, as busy servants bustled about attending to the wants of the numerous guests who ate and drank, sang, danced, and slept as they listed.

None but the lowly shepherds in the fields had taken note of them. To them happened a strange thing that night.

It must have been about midnight. The moon had crept slowly up the sky and flooded the hills with light. The oldest of the shepherds was on watch, while the others slept. Many things revolved in his mind—the promises to Abraham and to his seed forever—the words of peace that the traveller from Nazareth had spoken, swept through his memory. He began to dream. And the first thing that struck him was the strange behavior of the sheep in the folds. They rose from the ground and, facing toward the mountain, knelt as lambs kneel at their mothers' sides. But they were all still, as still as if carved of stone. And while he wondered, suddenly there stood near him—so suddenly that it was as if he had dropped down upon him—a presence. He had no time to question—a light—a glory unimaginable—brighter than the moon—more glorious than the sun—like the glory of the Lord. It awoke some of the others. It was round about them, and they were sore afraid. Then a voice sounded in their ears—and the angel said unto them: "Fear not; for behold: I bring you good tidings of great joy, which shall be to all people; for unto you is born this day in the city of David a Saviour, which is Christ the Lord. And this shall be a sign unto you: ye shall find the babe wrapped in swaddling clothes, lying in a manger."

Astonished and still terrified—stunned beyond thought—the shepherds lay as they had been found—and suddenly there was with the angel a multitude of the Heavenly host, praising God, and saying, "Glory to God in the Highest, and on earth peace to men of good will." Then they went away upward—up into Heaven—and only the shepherds were left on the earth with their flocks. When they recovered their courage and looked up, the sky was as usual on clear and cloudless nights—and only the moon was shining down, flooding the fields with light. They began to talk in low tones of what they had seen and heard, and to wonder what it all meant. . . . They were too wonder-struck—and presently they began to say one to another, "Let us now go even to Bethlehem and see this thing which is come to pass, which the Lord hath made known unto us."

"If we are going," said the leader, "we might as well take with us some milk. We may come across our friends, Joseph and his wife, and they will find it hard to get anything in that crowded place." He went off, and in a little while came back with a bottle of milk.

Out in the dusty road they filed, one behind the other, and by the moonlight began to ascend the winding, rocky road which led up toward the hills above them. Stumbling over the rocks in the dusk with their ill-shod feet; passing the commonplace wayfarers coming or going with their asses or on foot, it was hard to believe that but now

they had seen and heard Heavenly messengers—as Abraham and Jacob and Daniel had seen them.

"Well we shall know when we get there. If the babe be there—we shall know," said the leader.

It was near day when they reached the town. They came at length to the gate of the inn. In the twilight of the dawn it was just being opened by the sleepy and gruff porter as they arrived, and he stood in the open gateway yawning. He heard their inquiry in dull silence.

He pondered a moment. "What is it ye want?" he asked sullenly.

"We want to know if two travellers who came here late last night found shelter?"

"Two travellers? Nearer two hundred. Look at the courtyard. So full that one cannot walk across it. And the house is packed."

"Two who came late? A man and a young woman—he was much older than she—she—"

"Oh! Aye. Two came late—too late—"

"What became of them?"

"There was no place for them in the inn—"

"And you turned them away?"

"Who said I did?"

"What became of them?"

The porter half turned.

"Go look in there." He pointed toward the stable. "I gave them shelter there for the young woman—and none too soon. There are three of them there now, I judge, from what I heard but now."

The shepherds gave an exclamation and, passing across the courtyard to the stable, paused at the opening that led into the dusky recess. A woman's voice, low and soft, yet jubilant, was heard. She was speaking in the tone of gladness of a young mother:

"My soul doth magnify the Lord. And my spirit hath rejoiced in God my Saviour."

The shepherds approached softly, and there in the manger, wrapped in swaddling-bands, lay the young child.

It was, then, not a dream. This was the sign unto them.

"His mercy is on them that fear Him, from generation to generation," crooned the young mother as the shepherds drew near. "He hath put down the mighty from their seats and exalted them of low degree." It was

Painting by Grinnell showing the fear and awe felt by the shepherds. Painting copyright Ideals Publications Incorporated.

the hymn of the poor.

The shepherds entered softly. The morning light stole into the recess and fell on the group, and the shepherds sank to their knees to gaze on the babe in wondering awe. So, in the stable began the first worship of Him who came to save the world—Christ the Lord.

The Consecration of THE COMMON WAY

Edwin Markham

The hills that had been lone and lean
Were pricking with a tender green,
And flocks were whitening over them
From all the fields of Bethlehem.
The King of Heaven had come our way,
And in a lowly stable lay:
He had descended from the sky
In answer to the world's long cry—

Descended in a lyric burst
Of high archangels, going first
Unto the lowest and the least,
To humble bird and weary beast.
His palace was a wayside shed,

A battered manger was his bed;
An ox and ass with breathings deep
Made warm the chamber of his sleep.
Three sparrows with a friendly sound
Were picking barley from the ground;
An early sunbeam, long and thin,
Slanted across the dark within,
And brightened in its silver fall
A cart-wheel leaning to the wall.
An ox-yoke hung upon a hook;
A worn plow with a clumsy crook
Was lying idly by the wheel.
And everywhere there was the feel

Of that sweet peace that labor brings—
The peace that dwells with homely things.
Now have the homely things been made
Sacred, and a glory on them laid.
For He whose shelter was a stall,
The King was born among them all.
He came to handle saw and plane,
To use and hallow the profane:
Now is the holy not afar
In temples lighted by a star,
But where the loves and labors are.
Now that the King has gone this way,
Great are the things of every day.

A tender painting by Florence Kroger depicting the shepherds' arrival
at the manger. Painting copyright Ideals Publications Incorporated.

The SHEPHERDS

Samuel Taylor Coleridge

The shepherds went their hasty way,
And found the lowly stable-shed,
Where the virgin-mother lay:
And now they checked their eager tread,
For to the babe, that at her bosom clung,
A mother's song the virgin-mother sung.

They told her how a glorious light,
Streaming from a heavenly throng,
Around them shone, suspending night,
While, sweeter than a mother's song,
Blest angels heralded the Saviour's birth,
Glory to God on high! and peace on earth.

She listened to the tale divine,
And closer still the babe she pressed;
And while she cried, "The babe is mine!"
The milk rushed faster to her breast:
Joy rose within her, like a summer's morn;
Peace, peace on earth!
The Prince of peace is born.

A magnificent painting, ADORATION OF THE SHEPHERDS, by seventeenth-century painter Charles Le Brun, now in the Louvre, Paris, France. Photograph copyright Superstock.

Blessings of Magi

The Star

Patience Strong

Nigh two thousand years ago
Three seekers journeyed far—
Out into a distant country,
Following a star,
A star that blazed a trail of glory,
Shining like a gem—
Leading to the stable
Of an inn at Bethlehem.

There they found the manger
Where the infant Saviour lay.
Oh, that we poor travellers
Upon life's weary way
Might behold the Star of Christ
And have the faith to go—
Out into the world, believing,
Following its glow.

Once again the Christmas message
Rings around the earth—
Bringing men the glorious tidings
Of a Saviour's birth.
May His Star shine out upon
The darkened world today—
Lighting up the path of peace
And showing us the way.

ADORATION OF THE MAGI by fifteenth-century Italian painter Andrea Mantegna, now in the J.P. Getty Museum, Malibu, California. Photograph copyright Superstock.

Frankincense AND Myrrh

Heywood Broun

Once there were three kings in the East, and they were wise men. They read the heavens and they saw a certain strange star by which they knew that in a distant land the King of the World was to be born. The star beckoned to them and they made preparations for a long journey.

From their palaces they gathered rich gifts, gold and frankincense and myrrh. Great sacks of precious stuffs were loaded upon the backs of the camels which were to bear them on their journey. Everything was in readiness, but one of the wise men seemed perplexed and would not come at once to join his two companions, who were eager and impatient to be on their way in the direction indicated by the star.

They were old, these two kings, and the other wise man was young. When they asked him he could not tell why he waited. He knew that his treasures had been ransacked for rich gifts for the King of Kings. It seemed that there was nothing more which he could give, and yet he was not content.

He made no answer to the old men who shouted to him that the time had come. The camels were impatient and swayed and snarled. The shadows across the desert grew longer. And still the young king sat and thought deeply.

At length he smiled, and he ordered his servants to open the great treasure sack upon the back of the first of his camels. Then he went into a high chamber to which he had not been since he was a child. He rummaged about and presently came out and approached the caravan. In his hand he carried something which glinted in the sun.

The kings thought that he bore some new gift more rare and precious than any which they had been able to find in all their treasure rooms. They bent down to see, and even the camel drivers peered from the backs of the great beasts to find out what it was that gleamed in the sun. They were curious about this last gift for which all the caravan had waited.

And the young king took a toy from his hand and placed it upon the sand. It was a dog of tin, painted white and speckled with black spots. Great patches of paint had worn away and left the metal clear, and that was why the toy shone in the sun as if it were silver.

The youngest of the wise men turned a key in the side of the little black and white dog, and then he stepped aside so that the kings and the

camel drivers could see. The dog leaped high in the air and turned a somersault. He turned another and another and then fell over upon his side and lay there with a set and painted grin upon his face.

A child, the son of a camel driver, laughed and clapped his hands, but the kings were stern. They rebuked the youngest of the wise men, but he paid no attention and called to his chief servant to make the first of all the camels kneel. Then he picked up the toy of tin and, opening the treasure sack, placed his last gift with his own hands in the mouth of the sack so that it rested safely upon the soft bags of incense.

"What folly has seized you?" cried the eldest of the wise men. "Is this a gift to bear to the King of Kings in the far country?"

And the young man answered and said: "For the King of Kings there are great richness, gold and frankincense and myrrh.

"But this," he said, "is for the child in Bethlehem!"

A nineteenth-century Christmas greeting featuring the Adoration of the Magi. Photograph copyright Superstock.

A CAROL

Amy Carmichael

There are two Bethlehems in the land,
     Two little Bethlehems there.
O wise Men, do you understand
     To seek Him everywhere?
The heavenly Child lies holily,
The heavenly Child lies lowlily,
     No crown on His soft hair.

There are three crosses on the hill,
     Three dreadful crosses there,
And very dark and very chill,
     The heavy, shuddering air.
Is there a sign to show my Lord,
The sinner's Saviour, Heaven's Adored?
     'Tis He with thorn-crowned hair.

For in His lovely baby days
     Heaven's door was set ajar,
And angels flew through glimmering ways
     And lit a silver star.
No need for halo or for crown
To show the King of Love come down
     To dwell where sinners are.

But when He died upon the Rood,
     The King of glory, He,
There was no star, there was no good,
     Nor any majesty.
For diadem was only scorn,
A twisted, torturing crown of thorn.
     And it was all for me.

The Gift

Laura Spencer Portor

Caspar, Melchior, Balthazar,
These are they who followed the star.

Myrrh and incense, gems and gold,
These are the gifts they brought of old;—

These are the precious wonderful things
They brought, as befitting three wise Kings.

The humble Shepherds were quite too poor
To lay such gifts on the stable floor;

But one left his cloak and mittens; another
His shepherd's crook and cap; and his brother,

Who had carried a lamb across the wild,
Left that as a gift for the Holy Child.

Oh, Mary might better have liked a gem—
(For the best of women are fond of them)

And Joseph no doubt the gold approved;—
'Tis a thing men's hearts have always loved;

These things I suspect;—but sure I am
The Little Lord Christ preferred the lamb.

A winter scene in Topsham, Vermont, is pretty enough for a Christmas card. Photograph copyright Dick Dietrich.

The Man Who BROUGHT THE MYRRH

Shirley G. Robinson

The listening silence held its cold, sparkling arms about them, bringing Heaven close to the three tired travelers who, in spite of the excitement and wonder of the last few hours, had fallen asleep on the ground before the ebbing campfire.

Upon each countenance sleep carved a deep calmness, a serenity, a radiance which might be explained only by one who recognized the three as sages from the East who had just come from worship of the newly born King of the Jews.

Now they were on their way back to the king's palace to bring Herod news of the Child and of the place of His birth.

Beyond the hill, a shimmering white light began to appear slowly, steadily. As it became brighter, its radiance seemed to spread, illuminating the surrounding countryside. With a start, the travelers awakened and sat up as they heard a voice saying, "Behold."

Blinded by brilliance, the wise men gasped at the glory of the man appearing above them. Clothed in lustrous white robes, the figure seemed suspended on a path of light extending from the heavens. The sages uttered a cry of fear as of one man, and fell upon their faces.

Now in a gentle but penetrating voice, the angel spoke again: "Fear not, for behold! I come to you from the Father on high who has seen you this night in your worship of His Son, the Christ. I bring to you His message: Do not return to Herod with news of that which has just come to pass and which you have witnessed; for he is seeking the young child to destroy Him."

As suddenly as it had appeared, the light began to tremble and fade, and the angel rose into it and disappeared.

Now Herod waited many days for the return of the wise men. When he saw that he was bing mocked by them, he became exceedingly angry and sent for his messengers to seek the Child themselves.

While they sought diligently for the Child, Herod rent his clothes and tore out his hair in wrath and jealousy. He was now an old man, and knowing that his days upon the earth were numbered, he called together his chief priests. Suppose the throne should pass into the hands of this unknown "King of the Jews"? What would become of him in his last days and of his heirs?

By this time Joseph had been warned in a dream to take the Child and His mother and to flee into Egypt to remain until Herod's death.

Vainly seeking the Christ Child or word of Him, the messengers soon became weary and returned to the king, only to be sent forth again into all parts of Bethlehem and the coasts thereof with the command to slay every child of two years and under—according to the time at which Herod had first inquired of the wise men concerning the Child. The Child's destruction now seemed assured.

Before the return of the commissioner, however, Herod in his great wrath fell violently ill upon his bed and died, leaving the throne to his son.

And when Joseph had received this word from God, he took the Child Jesus and His mother into Galilee, making their dwelling in a place called Nazareth, that it might be fulfilled what was spoken by the prophets: "He shall be called a Nazarene.". . .

The threatening silence closed in about them, bringing heaven close to the crowd thronging about the hillside. Out of the silence a sudden cry of unimaginable anguish escaped the lips of One hanging from a rough-hewn cross at the crest of a hill.

Upon His countenance pain carved a deep calmness, a serenity, a radiance which could be explained most fully, perhaps, by an old man who slowly, haltingly, made his way through the mocking crowd to the foot of the hill, where he laid his gift of myrrh. Then he fell down, trembling, in worship of his King.

The crowd moved back in silence as the heavens grew darker and darker, and a deep peace settled over the face of the One hanging from the cross as He parted His lips for the final time. "Father, into Thy hands I commend my spirit."

ADORATION OF THE MAGI *painted by the sixteenth-century Italian Camillo Procaccini. Photograph copyright Superstock.*

The old man, tearfully, quietly, made his way back to the place where his camel waited.

Remembering a night years past, he thought of the two companions who had accompanied him to worship the Babe in the manger. What would they have thought if they could have witnessed the scene which he had just witnessed?

Perhaps they had, and were even now preparing their gifts of heavenly gold and frankincense to greet Him when He came home.

To the Three KINGS

Evelyn Waugh

How laboriously you came, taking sights and calculating
Where the shepherds had run barefoot!
Yet you came, and were not turned away.
For his sake, who did not reject your curious gifts,
Pray always for the learned, the oblique, the delicate.
Let them not be forgotten at the Throne of God
When the simple come into their Kingdom.

Dramatic painting of the Magi astride their camels following the star.
Painting copyright Ideals Publications Incorporated.

The Wise Men's Story

Lola S. Morgan

How shall we say if suddenly the sky
Were newly starred, or if our hearts were high
With visions of a destiny which led
Us on, although we questioned where and why?

We followed love, and we were comforted
On that long journey by a light which fed
Our souls with faith which did not fade nor die,
A light whose source lay on a manger bed.

We hoped to find a child, but did not know
He would be in a stable, poor and small,
But filled with joy so great it seemed to flow
Like music, making every dream grow tall.

We are three kings who sought a palace door,
But knelt, instead, to worship on a stable floor.

Christmas PRAYER

Peter Marshall

We yearn, our Father, for the simple beauty of Christmas—for all the old familiar melodies and words that remind us of that great miracle when He who had made all things was one night to come as a babe, to lie in the crook of a woman's arm.

Before such mystery we kneel, as we follow the shepherds and Wise Men to bring Thee the gift of our love—a love we confess has not always been as warm or sincere or real as it should have been. But now, on this Christmas Day, that love would find its Beloved, and from Thee receive the grace to make it pure again, warm and real.

We bring Thee our gratitude for every token of Thy love, for all the ways Thou hast heaped blessings upon us during the years that have gone.

And we do pray, Lord Jesus, that as we celebrate Thy birthday, we may do it in a manner well pleasing to Thee. May all we do and say, every tribute of our hearts, bring honor to Thy name, that we, Thy people, may remember Thy birth and feel Thy presence among us even yet.

May the loving kindness of Christmas not only creep into our hearts, but there abide, so that not even the return to earthly cares and responsibilities, not all the festivities of our own devising may cause it to creep away weeping. May the joy and spirit of Christmas stay with us now and forever.

In the name of Jesus, who came to save His people from their sins, even in that lovely name we pray. Amen.

Twilight falls over the village of Waits River, Vermont.
Photograph copyright Dick Dietrich Photography.

The Three Kings OF COLOGNE

Eugene Field

From out Cologne there came three kings
To worship Jesus Christ, their King.
To Him they sought, fine herbs they brought,
And many a beauteous golden thing;
They brought their gifts to Bethlehem town,
And in that manger set them down.

Then spake the first king, and he said:
"O Child, most heavenly, bright, and fair!
I bring this crown to Bethlehem town
For Thee, and only Thee, to wear;
So give a heavenly crown to me
When I shall come at last to Thee!"

The second, then. "I bring Thee here
This royal robe, O Child!" he cried;
"Of silk 'tis spun, and such a one
There is not in the world beside;
So in the day of doom requite
Me with a heavenly robe of white."

The third king gave his gift, and quoth:
"Spikenard and myrrh to Thee I bring,
And with these twain would I most fain
Anoint the body of my King;
So may their incense sometime rise
To plead for me in yonder skies!"

Thus spake the three kings of Cologne,
That gave their gifts and went away;
And now kneel I in prayer hard by
The cradle of the Child today;
Nor crown, nor robe, nor spice I bring
As offering unto Christ, my King.

Yet have I brought a gift the Child
May not despise, however small;
For here I lay my heart today,
And it is full of love to all.
Take Thou the poor but loyal thing,
My only tribute, Christ, my King!

This painting by an unknown artist depicts the Magi worshiping at the manger.
Painting copyright Ideals Publications Incorporated.

The Sign in THE SKY

Henry Van Dyke

In the days when Augustus Caesar was master of many kings, and Herod reigned in Jerusalem, there lived in the city of Ecbatana, among the mountains of Persia, a certain man named Artaban, the Median. His house stood close to the outermost of the seven walls which encircled the royal treasury. From his roof he could look over the rising battlements of black and white and crimson and blue and red and silver and gold to the hill where the summer palace of the Parthian emperors glittered like a jewel in a sevenfold crown.

Around the dwelling of Artaban spread a fair garden, a tangle of flowers and fruit trees, watered by a score of streams descending from the slopes of Mount Orontes, and made musical by innumerable birds. But all color was lost in the soft and odorous darkness of the late September night, and all sounds were hushed in the deep charm of its silence, save the plashing of the water, like a voice half sobbing and half laughing under the shadows. High above the trees a dim glow of light shone through the curtained arches of the upper chamber, where the master of the house was holding council with his friends.

He stood by the doorway to greet his guests—a tall, dark man of about forty years, with brilliant eyes set near together under his broad brow, and firm lines graven around his fine, thin lips; the brow of a dreamer and the mouth of a soldier, a man of sensitive feeling but inflexible will—one of those who, in whatever age they may live, are born for inward conflict and a life of quest.

His robe was of pure white wool, thrown over a tunic of silk; and a white, pointed cap with long lapels at the sides rested on his flowing black hair. It was the dress of the ancient priesthood of the Magi, called the fire-worshippers.

"Welcome!" he said, in his low, pleasant voice, as one after another entered the room—"Welcome, Abdus; peace be with you, Rhodaspes and Tigranes, and with you my father, Abgarus. You are all welcome, and this house grows bright with the joy of your presence."

There were nine of the men, differing widely in age, but alike in the richness of their dress of many-colored silks, and in the massive golden collars around their necks, marking them as Parthian nobles, and in the winged circles of gold resting upon their breasts, the sign of the followers of Zoroaster.

They took their places around a small black altar at the end of the room, where a tiny flame was burning. Artaban, standing beside it, and waving a barsom of thin tamarisk branches above the fire, fed it with dry sticks of pine and fragrant oils. Then he began the ancient chant of the Yasna, and the voices of his companions joined in the beautiful hymn to Ahura-Mazda:

We worship the Spirit Divine,
All wisdom and goodness possessing,
Surrounded by Holy Immortals,
The givers of bounty and blessing;
We joy in the works of His hands,
His truth and His power confessing. . . .

The fire rose with the chant, throbbing as if it were made of musical flame, until it cast a bright illumination through the whole apartment, revealing its simplicity and splendor.

The floor was laid with tiles of dark blue veined with white; pilasters of twisted silver stood out against the blue walls; the clearstory of round-arched windows above them was hung with azure silk; the vaulted ceiling was a pavement of sapphires, like the body of heaven in its clearness, sown with silver stars. From the four corners of the roof hung four golden magic-wheels, called the tongues of the gods. At the eastern end, behind the altar, there were two dark red pillars of porphyry; above them a lintel of the same stone, on which was carved the figure of a winged archer, with his arrow set to the string and his bow drawn.

The doorway between the pillars, which opened upon the terrace of the roof, was covered with a heavy curtain of the color of a ripe pomegranate, embroidered with innumerable golden rays shooting upward from the floor. In effect the room was like a quiet, starry night, all azure and silver, flushed in the east with the rosy promise of dawn. It was, as the house of a man should be, an expression of the character and spirit of the master.

He turned to his friends when the song was ended and invited them to be seated on the divan at the western end of the room.

"You have come tonight," said he, looking around the circle, "at my call, as the faithful scholars of Zoroaster, to renew your worship and rekindle your faith in the God of Purity, even as this fire has been rekindled on the altar. We worship not the fire, but Him of whom it is the chosen symbol, because it is the purest of all created things. It speaks to us of one who is Light and Truth. Is it not so, my father?"

"It is well said, my son," answered the venerable Abgarus. "The enlightened are never idolaters. They lift the veil of the form and go into the shrine of the reality, and new light and truth are coming to them continually through the old symbols."

"Hear me, then, my father and my friends," said Artaban, very quietly, "while I tell you of the new light and truth that have come to me through the most ancient of all signs. We have searched the secrets of nature together, and studied the healing virtues of water and fire and the plants. We have read also the books of prophecy in which the future is dimly foretold in words that are hard to understand. But the highest of all learning is the knowledge of the stars. To trace their courses is to untangle the threads of the mystery of life from the beginning to the end. If we could follow them perfectly, nothing would be hidden from us. But is not our knowledge of them still incomplete? Are there not many stars still beyond our horizon—lights that are known only to the dwellers in the far southland, among the spice trees of Punt and the gold mines of Ophir?"

There was a murmur of assent among

A colorful stained glass window of the Magi offering their gifts, Redeemer Lutheran Church, St. Paul, Minnesota. Photograph copyright The Crosiers, Gene Plaisted, OSC.

the listeners.

"The stars," said Tigranes, "are the thoughts of the Eternal. They are numberless. But the thoughts of man can be counted, like the years of his life. The wisdom of the Magi is the greatest of all wisdoms on earth, because it knows its own ignorance. And that is the secret of power. We keep men always looking and waiting for a new sunrise. But we ourselves know that the darkness is equal to the light, and that the conflict between them will never be ended."

"That is true," said the voice of Abgarus; "Every faithful disciple of Zoroaster knows the prophecy of the Avesta and carries the word in his heart: 'In that day Sosiosh the Victorious shall arise out of the number of the prophets in the east country. Around him shall shine a mighty brightness, and he shall make life everlasting, incorruptible, and immortal, and the dead shall rise again.'"

"This is a dark saying," said Tigranes, "and it may be that we shall never understand it. It is better to consider the things that are near at hand, and to increase the influence of the Magi in their own country, rather than to look for one who may be a stranger, and to whom we must resign our power."

The others seemed to approve these words. There was a silent feeling of agreement manifest among them; their looks responded with that indefinable expression which always follows when a speaker has uttered the thought that has been slumbering in the hearts of his listeners. But Artaban turned to Abgarus with a glow on his face, and said:

"My father, I have kept this prophecy in the secret place of my soul. Religion without a great hope would be like an altar without a living fire. And now the flame has burned more brightly, and by the light of it I have read other words which also have come from the fountain of Truth, and speak yet more clearly of the rising of the Victorious One in his brightness."

He drew from the breast of his tunic two small rolls of fine linen, with writing upon them, and unfolded them carefully upon his knee.

"In the years that are lost in the past, long before our fathers came into the land of Babylon, there were wise men in Chaldea, from whom the first of the Magi learned the secret of the heavens. And of these Balaam, the son of Beor, was one of the mightiest. Hear the words of his prophecy: '"There shall come a star out of Jacob, and a sceptre shall arise out of Israel.'"

The lips of Tigranes drew downward with contempt, as he said:

"Judah was a captive by the waters of Babylon, and the sons of Jacob were in bondage to our kings. The tribes of Israel are scattered through the mountains like lost sheep, and from the remnant that dwells in Judea under the yoke of Rome neither star nor sceptre shall arise."

"And yet," answered Artaban, "it was the Hebrew Daniel, the mighty searcher of dreams, the counselor of kings, the wise Bel-

teshazzar, who was most honored and beloved of our great King Cyrus. A prophet of sure things and a reader of the thoughts of God, Daniel proved himself to our people. And these are the words that he wrote." (Artaban read from the second roll:) "'Know, therefore, and understand that from the going forth of the commandment to restore Jerusalem, unto the Anointed One, the Prince, the time shall be seven and three-score and two weeks.'"

"But, my son," said Abgarus, doubtfully, "these are mystical numbers. Who can interpret them, or who can find the key that shall unlock their meaning?"

Artaban answered: "It has been shown to me and to my three companions among the Magi—Caspar, Melchior, and Balthazar. We have searched the ancient tablets of Chaldea and computed the time. It falls in this year. We have studied the sky, and in the spring of the year we saw two of the greatest stars draw near together in the sign of the Fish, which is the house of the Hebrews. We also saw a new star there, which shone for one night and then vanished. Now again the two great planets are meeting. This night is their conjunction. My three brothers are watching at the ancient Temple of the Seven Spheres, at Borsippa, in Babylonia, and I am watching here. If the star shines again, they will wait ten days for me at the temple, and then we will set out together for Jerusalem, to see and worship the promised one who shall be born King of Israel. I believe the sign will come. I have made ready for the journey. I have sold my house and my possessions, and bought these three jewels—a sapphire, a ruby, and a pearl—to carry them as tribute to the King. And I ask you to go with me on the pilgrimage, that we may have joy together in finding the Prince who is worthy to be served."

While he was speaking, he thrust his

hand into the inmost fold of his girdle and drew out three great gems—one blue as a fragment of the night sky, one redder than a ray of sunrise, and one as pure as the peak of a snowy mountain at twilight—and laid them on the outspread linen scrolls before him.

But his friends looked on with strange and alien eyes. A veil of doubt and mistrust came over their faces, like a fog creeping up from the marshes to hide the hills. They glanced at each other with looks of wonder and pity, as those who have listened to incredible sayings, the story of a wild vision, or the proposal of an impossible enterprise.

At last Tigranes said: "Artaban, this is a vain dream. It comes from too much looking upon the stars and the cherishing of lofty thoughts. It would be wiser to spend the time in gathering money for the new fire-temple at Chala. No king will ever rise from the broken race of Israel, and no end will ever come to the eternal strife of light and darkness. He who looks for it is a chaser of shadows. Farewell."

And another said: "Artaban, I have no knowledge of these things, and my office as guardian of the royal treasure binds me here. The quest is not for me. But if thou must follow it, fare thee well."

And another said: "In my house there sleeps a new bride, and I cannot leave her, nor take her with me on this strange journey. This quest is not for me. But may thy steps be prospered wherever thou goest. So, farewell."

And another said: "I am ill and unfit for hardship, but there is a man among my servants whom I will send with thee when thou goest, to bring me word how thou fairest."

But Abgarus, the oldest and the one who loved Artaban the best, lingered after the others had gone, and said, gravely: "My son, it may be that the light of truth is in this sign that has appeared in the skies, and then it will surely lead to the Prince and the mighty brightness. Or it may be that it is only a shadow of the light, as Tigranes has said, and then he who follows it will have only a long pilgrimage and an empty search. But it is better to follow even the shadow of the best than to remain content with the worst. And those who would see wonderful things must often be ready to travel alone. I am too old for this journey, but my heart shall be a companion of the pilgrimage day and night, and I shall know the end of thy quest. Go in peace."

So one by one they went out of the azure chamber with its silver stars, and Artaban was left in solitude.

He gathered up the jewels and replaced them in his girdle. For a long time he stood and watched the flame that flickered and sank upon the altar. Then he crossed the hall, lifted the heavy curtain, and passed out between the dull red pillars of porphyry to the terrace on the roof.

The shiver that thrills through the earth ere she rouses from her night sleep had already begun, and the cool wind that heralds the daybreak was drawing downward from the lofty, snow-traced ravines of Mount Orontes. Birds, half awakened, crept and chirped among the rustling leaves, and the smell of ripened grapes came in brief wafts from the arbors.

Far over the eastern plain a white mist stretched like a lake. But where the distant peak of Zagros serrated the western horizon, the sky was clear. Jupiter and Saturn rolled together like drops of lambent flame about to blend in one.

As Artaban watched them, behold— an azure spark was born out of the darkness beneath, rounding itself with purple splen-

The light radiates from the manger and illuminates the faces of the worshipping Magi. Painting by Peter Bianchi copyright Ideals Publications Incorporated.

dors to a crimson sphere, and spiring upward through rays of saffron and orange into a point of white radiance. Tiny and infinitely remote, yet perfect in every part, it pulsated in the enormous vault as if the three jewels in the Magician's breast had mingled and been transformed into a living heart of light.

He bowed his head. He covered his brow with his hands.

"It is the sign," he said. "The King is coming, and I will go to meet him."

Blessings of JESUS

Hamlet

William Shakespeare
I.i.158-164

Some say that ever 'gainst that season comes
Wherein our Saviour's birth is celebrated,
This bird of dawning singeth all night long,
And then they say no spirit dare stir abroad;
The nights are wholesome, then no planets strike,
No fairy takes, nor witch hath power to charm,
So hallowed, and so gracious, is that time.

To Come UNTO ME

Robert Nathan

That year there were very few houses for rent anywhere; and people lived wherever they could. Only the rich were able to buy an entire house, with wood and plaster walls, a rose garden and a bathroom. Nevertheless on Christmas Eve both rich and poor enjoyed the spirit of the season; for the rich gave each other gifts and the poor were delighted with the sight of the Christmas trees which, painted white, blue, and even green, and decorated with colored lights, twinkled everywhere along the public highways.

At the house of a very famous man a party was in progress. Since this man was the president of a motion picture studio, his guests were for the most part motion picture actors and actresses, which is to say that they were the most beautiful and famous people in the world. This did not make them as happy as might have been expected; they joined in the singing of Christmas carols with hearts no less lonely and empty than those of poor people who also wished to be loved.

Among these famous and beautiful people were two children, named Henry and Lettice. Everybody in the world knew what they looked like, what they talked like, what their favorite games were, what they wore and what they liked to eat. But what no one knew was what was in their hearts, because their hearts were the hearts of children.

And so, while the fiddles scraped, while the great singers sang, and while the footmen passed about among the guests with glasses of champagne and punch, and little sandwiches in the shape of snowflakes and crescent moons, and gingersnaps for the children, Lettice went tip-toeing to Henry in one corner of the great room and asked him, "What are you doing?"

To which Henry replied, "Nothing."

However, nothing to a child is so crowded with dreams as *nothing*. And so, when Lettice said, "I know a wonderful secret," Henry followed her out of the room and down the long hall and out into the garden, prepared for all the beautiful things without a name which he had been dreaming about.

But all he saw at the end of the garden was a kind of stable, with a little light over the door.

"I don't think that's so wonderful," said Henry.

"That's because you don't know," said Lettice.

"Don't know what?" asked Henry.

In answer, Lettice opened the door of the stable. And there, lying in a crib made of an old manger, was a baby.

"Now what do you think?" said Lettice triumphantly.

"I don't think it's wonderful at all," said Henry.

"Do you think maybe it's Baby Jesus?" asked Lettice.

"I don't know," said Henry. "I never saw it before."

"I wish it was Baby Jesus," said Lettice, "because then we could pray."

"You can pray if you want to," said Henry, "on account of you wouldn't know who it was till afterward anyhow."

"I can say 'Now I lay me' and the Lord's Prayer," said Lettice.

"All right," said Henry. "I don't mind."

So the two children knelt on the floor of the tool shed, in front of the baby, whose father and mother, having no other place to live at the moment, were helping the cook at the big house wash dishes in return for a roof over their heads.

"Our Father which art in Heaven," said Lettice. "Hallowed be Thy name. . . ."

And all around them as they knelt, the invisible air was peopled with the unseen faces of the past, with saints and captains, beggars and kings, with the smiling children, the dreaming children into whose hands, year after year, God had delivered His world, into whose hearts, endlessly renewed, He had put His love, into whose keeping He had given His Son. . . .

"I pray the Lord," said Henry, "my soul to keep."

In the big house they sang "O Little Star of Bethlehem" and Lettice's mother and Henry's father wondered where they were. And in the kitchen the two new helpers smiled at each other across the soapy water. They did not expect very much for their child. Perhaps he might grow up to be a good carpenter.

Dawn on Christmas Day rises fair and clear over a barn in LaSalle County, Illinois. Photograph copyright Terry Donnelly.

Hymn on the Morning OF CHRIST'S NATIVITY

John Milton

It was the winter wild,
While the heaven-born child
All meanly wrapt in the rude manger lies;
Nature, in awe to him,
Had doffed her gaudy trim,
With her great Master so to sympathize:
It was no season then for her
To wanton with the sun, her lusty paramour.

Only with speeches fair
She woos the gentle air
To hide her guilty front with innocent snow,
And on her naked shame,
Pollute with sinful blame,
The saintly veil of maiden white to throw;
Confounded, that her Maker's eyes
Should look so near upon her foul deformities.

But he, her fears to cease,
Sends down the meek-eyed Peace;
She, crowned with olive green, came softly sliding
Down through the turning sphere,
His ready harbinger,
With turtle wing the amorous clouds dividing;
And waving wide her myrtle wand,
She strikes a universal peace through sea and land.

The stars, with deep amaze,
Stand fixed in steadfast gaze,
Bending one way their precious influence,
And will not take their flight,
For all the morning light,
Or Lucifer that often warned them thence;
But in their glimmering orbs did glow,
Until their Lord himself bespake and bid them go.

And though the shady gloom
Had given day her room,
The sun himself withheld his wonted speed,
And hid his head for shame,
As his inferior flame
The new-enlightened world no more should need:
He saw a greater Sun appear
Than his bright throne or burning axletree could bear.

*A blazing sun rises on a wonderful Christmas morning and reminds us of the Son that brought hope to all
mankind. Photograph copyright Superstock.*

The Holy
BIRTH

Jim Bishop

Joseph had run out of prayers and promises. His face was sick, his eyes listless. He looked up toward the east, and his dark eyes mirrored a strange thing: three stars, coming over the Mountains of Moab, were fused into one tremendously bright one. His eyes caught the glint of bright blue light, almost like a tiny moon, and he wondered about it and was still vaguely troubled by it when he heard a tiny, thin wail, a sound so slender that one had to listen again for it to make sure.

He wanted to rush inside at once. He got to his feet, and he moved no further. She would call him. He would wait. Joseph paced up and down, not realizing that men had done this thing for centuries before he was born, and would continue it for many centuries after he had gone.

"Joseph." It was a soft call, but he heard it. At once, he picked up the second jar of water and hurried inside. The two lamps still shed a soft glow over the stable, even though it seemed years since they had been lighted.

The first thing he noticed was his wife. Mary was sitting tailor-fashion with her back against a manger wall. Her face was clean; her hair had been brushed. There were blue hollows under her eyes. She smiled at her husband and nodded. Then she stood.

She beckoned him to come closer. Joseph, mouth agape, followed her to a little manger. It had been cleaned but, where the animals had nipped the edges of the wood, the boards were worn and splintered. In the manger were the broad bolts of white swaddling she had brought on the trip. They were doubled underneath and over the top of the baby.

Mary smiled at her husband as he bent far over to look. There, among the cloths, he saw the tiny face of an infant. This, said Joseph to himself, is the one of whom the angel spoke. He dropped to his knees beside the manger. This was the Messiah.

Nativity scene with an illuminated border painted by seventeenth-century artist Bartolome Esteban Murillo. Photograph copyright Superstock.

Christ's Nativity

Henry Vaughan

Awake, glad heart! Get up and sing!
It is the birth-day of thy King.
Awake! awake! The sun doth shake
Light from his locks, and, all the way
Breathing perfumes, doth spice the day.

Awake, awake! Hark how th' wood rings;
Winds whisper, and the busy springs
A concert make. Awake! awake!
Man is their high-priest, and should rise
To offer up the sacrifice.

I would I were some bird, or star,
Flutt'ring in woods, or lifted far
Above this inn and road of sin!
Then either star or bird should be
Shining or singing still to thee.

I would I had in my best part
Fit room for thee! Or that my heart
Were clean as thy manger was!
But I am all filth, and obscene;
Yet, if thou wilt, thou canst make me clean.

Sweet Jesu! I will then. Let no more
This leper haunt and soil thy door!
Cure him, ease him, O release him!
And let once more, by mystic birth,
The Lord of life be born in earth.

A Hymn for the NATIVITY OF MY SAVIOUR

Ben Jonson

I sing the birth was born tonight,
The Author both of life and light;
The angels so did sound it.
And like the ravished shepherds said,
Who saw the light and were afraid,
Yet searched, and true they found it.

The Son of God, the eternal King,
That did us all salvation bring,
And free the soul from danger;
He whom the whole world could not take,
The Word which heaven and earth did make,
Was now laid in a manger.

The Father's wisdom willed it so,
The Son's obedience knew no No,
Both wills were in one stature:
And as that wisdom had decreed,
The Word was now made flesh indeed,
And took on Him our nature.

What comfort by Him do we win,
Who made Himself the price for sin,
To make us heirs of Glory!
To see this Babe all innocence,
A martyr born in our defence;
Can man forget this story?

Another beautiful sunrise full of promise and hope over the Sawtooth Mountains near Stanley, Idaho.
Photograph copyright Dick Dietrich Photography.

The Maid-Servant
AT THE INN

Dorothy Parker

"It's queer," she said, "I see the light
As plain as I beheld it then,
All silver-like and calm and bright—
We've not had stars like that again!

"And she was such a gentle thing
To birth a baby in the cold.
The barn was dark and frightening—
This new one's better than the old.

"I mind my eyes were full of tears,
For I was young, and quick distressed,
But she was less than me in years
That held a son against her breast.

"I never saw a sweeter child—
The little one, the darling one!—
I mind I told her, when he smiled
You'd know he was his mother's son.

"It's queer that I should see them so—
The time they came to Bethlehem
Was more than thirty years ago;
I've prayed that all is well with them."

The Vigil of
JOSEPH

Elsa Barker

After the Wise Men went, and the strange star
Had faded out, Joseph the father sat
Watching the sleeping Mother and the Babe,
And thinking stern, sweet thoughts the long night through.
"Ah, what am I, that God has chosen me
To bear this blessed burden, to endure
Daily the presence of this loveliness,
To guide this Glory that shall guide the world?
Brawny these arms to win Him bread, and broad
This bosom to sustain her. But my heart
Quivers in lonely pain before that Beauty
It loves—and serves—and cannot understand!"

A painting by Joe Maniscalco that depicts the Holy Family at home. Painting copyright Ideals Publications Incorporated.

One Small
CHILD

Esther S. Buckwalter

One little child . . . no more, no less—
And could His mother Mary guess
Salvation for the human race
Depended on that night, that place?
And did she know this child would cause
All heaven to rock with glad applause?

Would cause the angels to rehearse
Their midnight song of sacred verse?
Would cause a star of strange design
To leave its orbit, and to shine

A brilliant path, from east to west?
Would cause wise men to choose the best
Of hoarded treasure, and to search
The nations from a camel perch?

Would make a king (in craven fear)
Destroy small man-children near?
To this small child the nation thrilled,
For He was prophecy fulfilled.

But could His mother even guess,
While rocking Him with tenderness,
The whole import of His advent,
This one small child—from heaven sent.

Painting of Mary and Baby Jesus by Florence Kroger. Painting copyright Ideals Publications Incorporated.

Guests

Author Unknown

Yet if his majesty, our sovereign lord,
    Should of his own accord
    Friendly himself invite,
And say, "I'll be your guest tomorrow night,"
How should we stir ourselves, call and command
All hands to work! "Let no man idle stand!

"Set me fine Spanish tables in the hall;
    See they be fitted all;
    Let there be room to eat
And order taken that there want no meat.
See every sconce and candlestick made bright,
That without tapers they may give a light.

"Look to the presence: are the carpets spread,
    The dazie o'er the head,
    The cushions in the chairs,
And all the candles lighted on the stairs?
Perfume the chambers, and in any case
Let each man give attendance in his place!"

Thus, if the king were coming would we do;
    And 'twere good reason too;
    For 'tis a duteous thing
To show all honor to an earthly king,
And after all our travail and our cost,
So he be pleased, to think no labor lost.

But at the coming of the King of Heaven
    All's set at six and seven:
    We wallow in our sin.
Christ cannot find a chamber in the inn.
We entertain him always like a stranger,
And, as at first, still lodge him in the manger.

Inasmuch

Heywood Broun

Once there lived near Bethlehem a man named Simon and his wife Deborah. And Deborah dreamed a curious dream, a dream so vivid that it might better be called a vision. It was not yet daybreak, but she roused her husband and told him that an angel had come to her in the vision and had said, as she remembered it, "Tomorrow night in Bethlehem the King of the World will be born." The rest was not so vivid in Deborah's mind, but she told Simon that wise men and kings were already on their way to Bethlehem, bringing gifts for the wonder child.

"When he is born," she said, "the wise men and the kings who bring these gifts will see the stars dance in the heavens and hear the voices of angels. You and I must send presents too, for this child will be the greatest man in all the world."

Simon objected that there was nothing of enough value in the house to take to such a child, but Deborah replied, "The King of the World will understand." Then, although it was not yet light, she got up and began to bake a cake, and Simon went beyond the town to the hills to get holly and made a wreath. Later in the day husband and wife looked over all their belongings, but the only suitable gift they could find was an old toy, a somewhat battered wooden duck that had belonged to their eldest son, who had grown up and married and gone away to live in Galilee. Simon painted the toy duck as well as he could, and Deborah told him to take it and the cake and the wreath of holly and go to Bethlehem. "It's not much," she said, "but the King will understand."

It was almost sunset when Simon started down the winding road that led to Bethlehem. Deborah watched him round the first turn and would have watched longer except that he was walking straight toward the sun and the light hurt her eyes. She went back into the house and an hour had hardly passed when she heard Simon whistling in the garden. He was walking very slowly. At the door he hesitated for almost a minute. She looked up when he came in. He was empty-handed.

"You haven't been to Bethlehem," said Deborah.

"No," said Simon.

"Then where is the cake, and the holly wreath, and the toy duck?"

"I'm sorry," said Simon, "I couldn't help it somehow. It just happened."

"What happened?" asked Deborah sharply.

"Well," said Simon, "just after I went around the first turn in the road I found a child sitting on that big white rock, crying. He was about

Holly has become a traditional decorating greenery. Photograph copyright Gene Ahrens.

two or three years old, and I stopped and asked him why he was crying. He didn't answer. Then I told him not to cry like that, and I patted his head, but that didn't do any good. I hung around, trying to think up something, and I decided to put the cake down and take him up in my arms for a minute. But the cake slipped out of my hands and hit the rock, and a piece of the icing chipped off. Well, I thought, that baby in Bethlehem won't miss a little piece of icing, and I gave it to the child and he stopped crying. But when he finished he began to cry again. I just sort of squeezed another little piece of icing off, and that was all right, for a little while; but then I had to give him another piece, and things went on that way, and all of a sudden I found that there wasn't any cake left. After that he looked as if he might cry again, and I didn't have any more cake and so I showed him the duck and he said 'Ta-ta.' I just meant to lend him the duck for a minute, but he wouldn't give it up. I coaxed him a good while, but he wouldn't let go. And then a woman came out of that little house and she began to scold him for staying out so late, and I told her it was my fault and I gave her the holly wreath just so she wouldn't be made at the child. And after that, you see, I didn't have anything to take to Bethlehem, and so I

came back here."

Deborah had begun to cry before Simon finished his story, but when he had done she lifted up her head and said, "How could you do it, Simon? Those presents were meant for the King of the World, and you gave them to the first crying child you met on the road."

Then she began to cry again, and Simon didn't know what to say or do, and it grew darker in the room and the fire on the hearth faded to a few embers. And that little red glow was all there was in the room. Now, Simon could not even see Deborah across the room, but he could still hear her sobbing. But suddenly the room was flooded with light and Deborah's sobbing broke into a great gulp and she rushed to the window and looked out. The stars danced in the sky and from high above the house came the voice of angels saying, "Glory to God in the highest, and on earth peace, good will toward men."

Deborah dropped to her knees in a panic of joy and fear. Simon knelt beside her, but first he said, "I thought maybe that the baby in Bethlehem wouldn't mind so very much."

John Walter

The Child
JESUS

Francis Quarles

Hail, blessed Virgin, full of heavenly grace,
Blest above all that sprang from human race;
Whose heaven-saluted womb brought forth in one
A blessed Saviour, and a blessed son:
O! what a ravishment 't had been to see
Thy little Saviour perking on thy knee!
To see him nuzzle in thy virgin breast!
His milk-white body all unclad, undrest;
To see thy busy fingers clothe and wrap
His spradling limbs in thy indulgent lap!
To see his desperate eyes, with childish grace,
Smiling upon his smiling mother's face!
And, when his forward strength began to bloom,
To see him diddle up and down the room!
O, who would think so sweet a babe as this
Should e'er be slain by a false-hearted kiss!

*For unto us a child is born, unto us a son is given: and
the government shall be upon his shoulder: and his
name shall be called Wonderful, Counsellor, The
mighty God, The everlasting Father, The Prince of
Peace. Of the increase of his government and peace
there shall be no end, upon the throne of David, and
upon his kingdom, to order it, and to establish it with
judgment and with justice from henceforth even for
ever. The zeal of the LORD of hosts will perform this.*
Isaiah 9:6-7

*Painting by John Walter shows the tenderness and love of the Holy Family.
Painting copyright Ideals Publications Incorporated.*

After Christmas a Landlord Remembers

Elizabeth Coatsworth

All day my wife, the maids, the men
And I ran to and fro,
What had been done we did again,
We served both high and low.

At last we lay in weary beds,
Then boomed a staff on door,
"O Landlord, here's a desperate head!"
The inn could hold no more.

He took her to the stable near,
I woke before the day,
For with her cry our cock crowed clear,
The little ass did bray.

There seemed to come a sound of song,
I could not get to sleep,
And then the shepherds came along
And brought their bleating sheep.

That meant more runnings to and fro,
More things to eat and drink,
The work was hard, the pay was low,
We had no time to drink.

With beasts rejoicing, peering swains,
Guests calling, new-born boys,
It was enough to turn our brains
Run-running through the noise.

Then came the kings with camels, too,
And horses white as milk,
And all their gorgeous retinue
Clad in brocades and silk.

The star that troubled us by night
Had led them all the way.
We worked like mad, but it was right—
At least the kings would pay.

All's past, we've time to take our ease
And try to figure out
Why our old ox fell to his knees
And what it was about.

She looked like any maid at all
Brought to her labor here,
But there's gold buried near the wall
And the beasts still act queer.

Who Can Forget?

Giles Fletcher

Who can forget—never to be forgot—
The time, that all the world in slumber lies,
When, like the stars, the singing angels shot
To earth, and heaven awakèd all his eyes
To see another sun at midnight rise
  On earth? Was never sight of pareil fame,
  For God before, man like Himself did frame,
But God Himself now like a mortal man became.

And yet but newly He was infanted,
And yet already He was sought to die;
Yet scarcely born, already banishèd;
Not able yet to go, and forced to fly;
But scarcely fled away, when by and by,
  The tyrant's sword with blood is all defil'd,
  And Rachel, for her sons with fury wild,
Cries, "O thou cruel king, and O my sweetest child!"

Egypt His nurse became, where Nilus springs,
Who straight, to entertain the rising sun,
The hasty harvest in his bosom brings;
But now for drought the fields were all undone,
And now with waters all is overrun;
  So fast the Cynthian mountains pour'd their snow
  When once they felt the sun so near them glow
That Nilus Egypt lost, and to a sea did grow.

The angels carolled loud their song of peace,
The cursèd oracles were stricken dumb;
To see their Shepherd the poor shepherds press,
To see their King the kingly sophies come;
And them to guide unto his Master's home,
  A star comes dancing up the orient,
  That springs for joy over the strawy tent,
Where gold, to make their Prince a crown, they all present.

Christmas Day

Edmund Hamilton Sears

Calm on the listening ear of night
Come heaven's melodious strains,
Where wild Judea stretches far
Her silver-mantled plains;
Celestial choirs from courts above
Shed sacred glories there,
And angels, with their sparkling lyres,
Make music on the air.

The answering hills of Palestine
Send back the glad reply,
And greet from all their holy heights
The dayspring from on high:
O'er the blue depths of Galilee
There comes a holier calm,
And Sharon waves in solemn praise
Her silent groves of palm.

Glory to God! the lofty strain
The realm of ether fills;
How sweeps the song of solemn joy
O'er Judah's sacred hills!
"Glory to God!" the sounding skies
Loud with their anthems ring:
"Peace on earth, goodwill to men,
From heaven's eternal King."

Light on thy hills, Jerusalem!
The Savior now is born:
More bright on Bethlehem's joyous plains
Breaks the first Christmas morn;
And brighter on Moriah's brow,
Crowned with her temple spires,
Which first proclaim the newborn light,
Clothed with its orient fires.

This day shall Christian tongues be mute,
And Christian hearts be cold?
O catch the anthem that from heaven
O'er Judah's mountains rolled!
When nightly burst from seraph harps
The high and solemn lay—
"Glory to God, on earth be peace;
Salvation comes today!"

Sunrise over the frozen coast. Photograph copyright Superstock.

Blessings of PEACE

The Stable Door

Patience Strong

They came that night to Bethlehem,
The simple and the wise.
The shepherd and the scholar
Saw the glory in the skies—
And sought the holy manger bed,
That place of mystery—
Where God Himself had broken in
Upon humanity.

The greatest men who walk the earth
Can offer us today—
No diviner revelation.
This then is the Way. . . .
Though to knowledge high and vast
The human mind may soar,
Every man must come at last
Unto the stable door.

ADORATION OF THE SHEPHERDS by the seventeenth-century painter Charles Le Brun, now in the Louvre, Paris, France. Photograph copyright SuperStock.

A Prayer—
For the Day
AFTER CHRISTMAS

Peter Marshall

O Lord Jesus, we thank Thee for the joys of this season, for the divine love that was shed abroad among men when Thou didst first come as a little child.

But may we not think of Thy coming as a distant event that took place once and has never been repeated. May we know that Thou art still here walking among us, by our sides, whispering over our shoulders, tugging at our sleeves, smiling upon us when we need encouragement and help.

We thank Thee for Thy spirit that moves at this season
    the hearts of men:
to be kindly and thoughtful—where before they were
    careless and indifferent,
to be generous—where before they lived in selfishness,
to be gentle—where before they had been rough and
    unmindful of the weak,
to express their love—where before it had been taken
    for granted and assumed.

We are learning, O Lord, so slowly—life's true values. Surely Christmas would teach us the unforgettable lesson of the things that matter most—the ties that bind the structure of the family upon which our country and all the world rests; the love that we have for one another which binds Thy whole creation to Thy footstool, Thy throne. We are learning slowly, but, O God, we thank Thee that we are learning.

So may Christmas linger with us, even as Thou art beside us the whole year through. Amen.

An historic round church decorated for the Christmas season in Richmond, Vermont. Photograph copyright Johnson's Photography.

Our Lady's JUGGLER

Anatole France

In the days when the world was young, there lived in France a man of no importance. Everyone said he was a man of no importance, and he firmly believed this himself. For he was just a poor traveling juggler, who could not read or write, who went about from town to town following the little country fairs and performing his tricks for a few pennies a day. His name was Barnaby.

When the weather was beautiful, and people were strolling about the streets, this juggler would find a clear space in the village square, spread a strip of old carpet out on the cobblestones, and on it perform his tricks for children and grown-ups alike. Now Barnaby, although he knew he was a man of no importance, was an amazing juggler.

First he would only balance a tin plate on the tip of his nose. But when the crowd had collected, he would stand on his hands and juggle six copper balls in the air at the same time, catching them with his feet. And sometimes, when he would juggle twelve sharp knives in the air, the villagers would be so delighted that a rain of pennies would fall on his strip of carpet. And when his day's work was over, and he was wearily resting his aching muscles, Barnaby would collect the pennies in his hat, kneel down reverently, and thank God for the gift.

Always the people would laugh at his simplicity and everyone would agree that Barnaby would never amount to anything. But all this is about the happy days in Barnaby's life, the springtime days when people were willing to toss a penny to a poor juggler. When winter came, Barnaby had to wrap his juggling equipment in the carpet, and trudge along the roads begging a night's lodging in farmers' barns, or entertaining the servants of some rich nobleman to earn a meal. And Barnaby never thought of complaining—he knew that the winter and the rains were as necessary as the spring sunshine, and he accepted his lot. "For how," Barnaby would say to himself as he trudged along, "could such an ignorant fellow as myself hope for anything better?"

And one year in France there was a terrible winter. It began to rain in October, and there was hardly a blue sky to be seen by the end of November. And on an evening in early December at the end of a dreary, wet day, as Barnaby trudged along a country road, sad and bent, carrying under his arm the golden balls and knives wrapped up in his old carpet, he met a monk. Riding a find white mule, dressed in warm clothes, well fed and comfortable, the monk smiled at the sight of Barnaby and called to him: "It's going to be cold before morning. How would you like to spend the night at the monastery?"

And that night Barnaby found himself seated in the great candlelit dining hall of the monastery. Although he sat at the bottom of the long table, together with the servants and beggars, Barnaby thought he had never seen such a wonderful sight in his life—the shining faces of fifty monks relaxing after this day of work and prayer.

Barnaby did not dare to suggest that he should perform his tricks, as they would be sacrilege before such men; but as he ate and drank more than he had ever had at a meal for years, a great resolution came over him. Although it made him tremble at his own boldness, as the meal ended, Barnaby suddenly arose, ran around the table down to where the lordly abbot sat at the head, and sank to his knees. "Father, grant my prayer! Let me stay in this wonderful place and work for you! I cannot hope to become one of you, I am too ignorant; but let me work in the kitchen and the fields and worship with you in the chapel!"

The monk who had met Barnaby on the road turned to the abbot: "This is a good man, simple and pure of heart." So the abbot nodded, and Barnaby that night put his juggling equipment under a cot in his own cubicle, and decided that never again would he go back to his old profession.

And in the days that followed, everyone smiled at the eager way he scrubbed the floors and labored throughout the buildings, and everyone smiled at his simplicity. As for Barnaby, his face shone with happiness from morning until night.

Until two weeks before Christmas—then Barnaby's joy suddenly turned to mis-

ery. For around him he saw every man preparing a wonderful gift to place in the chapel on Christmas—Brother Maurice, who had the art of illuminating copies of the Bible, and Brother Marbode, who was com-

Stained glass window depicting the birth of Jesus in Fron Lutheran Church, Starbuck, Minnesota. Photograph copyright The Crosiers, Gene Plaisted, OSC.

Ornate detail is a hallmark of the art of illumination. Copyright Ideals Publications Incorporated.

pleting a marvelous statue of Christ. Brother Ambrose, who wrote music, had completed the scoring of a great hymn to be played on the organ during Christmas services.

All about Barnaby those educated, trained artists followed their work, each one of them readying a beautiful gift to dedicate to God on Christmas Day. And what about Barnaby? He could do nothing. "I am but a rough man, unskilled in the arts, and I can write no book, offer no painting or statue or poem. Alas, I have no talent, I have no gift worthy of the day!"

So Barnaby sank deep into sadness and despair. Christmas Day came, and the chapel was resplendent with the gifts of the brothers. The giant organ rang with the new music; the choir sang the chorales; the candles glittered around the great new statue. And Barnaby was not there. He was in his tiny cubicle, praying forgiveness for having no gift to offer.

Then a strange thing happened. On the evening of Christmas Day, when the chapel should have been deserted, one of the monks came running, white-faced and panting with exertion, into the private office of the abbot. He threw open the door without knocking, and seized the abbot by the arms. "Father, a frightful thing is happening. The most terrible sacrilege ever to take place is going on right in our own chapel! Come!"

Together the two portly men ran down the corridors, burst through a door, and came out on the balcony at the rear of the chapel. The monk pointed down toward the altar. The abbot looked and turned ashen in color. "He is mad!"

For down below, in front of the altar, was Barnaby. He had spread out his strip of carpet and, kneeling reverently upon it, was actually juggling in the air twelve golden balls! He was giving his old performance, and giving it beautifully—his bright knives, the shining balls, the tin plate balanced on the tip of his nose. And on his face was a look of adoration and joy.

"We must seize him at once," cried the abbot, and turned for the door. But at that moment a light filled the church, a brilliant beam of light coming directly from the altar. Both monks sank to their knees.

For as Barnaby knelt exhausted on his carpet, they saw the statue of the Virgin Mary move. She stepped down from her pedestal, and coming to where Barnaby knelt, took the blue hem of her robe and touched it to his forehead, gently drying the perspiration that glistened there. Then the light dimmed. Up in the choir balcony the monk looked at his superior: "God accepted the only gift he had to make."

And the abbot slowly nodded: "Blessed are the poor in spirit, for theirs is the kingdom of heaven."

Madonna and Child window, St. Thomas Apostle Church, Corcoran, Minnesota. Photograph copyright The Crosiers, Gene Plaisted, OSC.

The Birth of
JESUS

Matthew 1:18-25, Luke 2:1-20, Matthew 2:1-15

Now the birth of Jesus Christ was on this wise: When as his mother Mary was espoused to Joseph, before they came together, she was found with child of the Holy Ghost. Then Joseph her husband, being a just man, and not willing to make her a publick example, was minded to put her away privily.

But while he thought on these things, behold, the angel of the Lord appeared unto him in a dream, saying, Joseph, thou son of David, fear not to take unto thee Mary thy wife: for that which is conceived in her is of the Holy Ghost. And she shall bring forth a son, and thou shalt call his name JESUS: for he shall save his people from their sins. Now all this was done, that it might be fulfilled which was spoken of the Lord by the prophet, saying, Behold, a virgin shall be with child, and shall bring forth a son, and they shall call his name Emmanuel, which being interpreted is, God with us. Then Joseph being raised from sleep did as the angel of the Lord had bidden him, and took unto him his wife: And knew her not till she had brought forth her firstborn son: and he called his name JESUS.

And it came to pass in those days, that there went out a decree from Caesar Augustus, that all the world should be taxed. . . . And all went to be taxed, every one into his own city. And Joseph also went up from Galilee, out of the city of Nazareth, into Judaea, unto the city of David, which is called Bethlehem; (because he was of the house and lineage of David:) To be taxed with Mary his espoused wife, being great with child. And so it was, that, while they were there, the days were accomplished that she should be delivered. And she brought forth her firstborn son, and wrapped him in swaddling clothes, and laid him in a manger; because there was no room for them in the inn.

And there were in the same country shepherds abiding in the field, keeping watch over their flock by night. And, lo, the angel of the Lord came upon them, and the glory of the Lord shone round about them: and they were sore afraid. And the angel said unto them, Fear not: for, behold, I bring you good tidings of great joy, which shall be to all people. For unto you is born this day in the city of David a Saviour, which is Christ the Lord. And this shall be a sign unto you; Ye shall find the babe wrapped in swaddling clothes, lying in a manger. And suddenly there was with the angel a multitude of the heavenly host praising God, and saying, Glory to God in the highest, and on earth peace, good will toward men. And it came to pass, as the angels were gone away from them into heaven, the shepherds said one to another, Let us now go even unto Bethlehem, and see this thing which is come to pass, which the Lord hath made known unto us. And they came with haste, and found Mary, and Joseph, and the babe lying in a manger. And when they had seen it, they made known abroad the saying which was told them concerning this child. And all they that heard it wondered at those things which were told them by the shepherds. But Mary kept all these things, and pondered them in her heart. And the shepherds returned, glorifying and praising God for all the things that they had heard and seen, as it was told unto them.

Now when Jesus was born in Bethlehem of Judaea in the days of Herod the king, behold, there came wise men from the east to Jerusalem, Saying, Where is he that is born King of the Jews? for we have seen his star in the east, and are come to worship him.

When Herod the king had heard these things, he was troubled. . . . And when he had

Joseph, seeking shelter, was offered only the stable. Painting by Joe Maniscalco copyright Ideals Publications Incorporated.

gathered all the chief priests and scribes of the people together, he demanded of them where Christ should be born. And they said unto him, In Bethlehem of Judaea: for thus it is written by the prophet, And thou Bethlehem, in the land of Juda, art not the least among the princes of Juda: for out of thee shall come a Governor, that shall rule my people Israel.

Then Herod, when he had privily called the wise men, inquired of them diligently what time the star appeared. And he sent them to Bethlehem, and said, Go and search diligently for the young child; and when ye have found him, bring me word again, that I may come and worship him also. When they had heard the king, they departed; and, lo, the star, which they saw in the east, went before them, till it came and stood over where the young child was. When they saw the star, they rejoiced with exceeding great joy.

And when they were come into the house, they saw the young child with Mary his mother, and fell down, and worshipped him: and when they had opened their treasures, they presented unto him gifts; gold, and frankincense, and myrrh. And being warned of God in a dream that they should not return to Herod, they departed into their own country another way. And when they were departed, behold, the angel of the Lord appeareth to Joseph in a dream, saying, Arise, and take the young child and his mother, and flee into Egypt, and be thou there until I bring thee word: for Herod will seek the young child to destroy him. When he arose, he took the young child and his mother by night, and departed into Egypt: And was there until the death of Herod: that it might be fulfilled which was spoken of the Lord by the prophet, saying, Out of Egypt have I called my son.

FLIGHT INTO EGYPT *by eighteenth-century artist John Martin. Photograph copyright Christie's Images/Superstock.*

A Ballad of CHRISTMAS

Walter de la Mare

It was about the deep of night,
　　And still was earth and sky,
When 'neath the moonlight dazzling bright,
　　Three ghosts came riding by.

Beyond the sea, beyond the sea,
　　Lie kingdoms for them all:
I wot their steeds trod wearily—
　　The journey was not small.

By rock and desert, sand and stream,
　　They footsore late did go:
Now like a sweet and blessed dream
　　Their path was deep with snow.

Shining like hoar-frost rode they on,
　　Three ghosts in earth's array;
It was about the hour when wan
　　Night turns at hint of day.

Oh, but their hearts with woe distraught
　　Hailed not the wane of night,
Only for Jesu still they sought
　　To wash them clean and white.

For bloody was each hand, and dark
　　With death each orbless eye;—
It was three traitors mute and stark
　　Came riding silent by.

Silver their raiment and their spurs,
　　And silver-shod their feet,
And silver-pale each face that stares
　　Into the moonlight sweet.

And he upon the left that rode
　　Was Pilate, Prince of Rome,
Whose journey once lay far abroad
　　And now was nearing home.

And he upon the right that rode
　　Herod of Salem sate,
Whose mantle dipped in children's blood
　　Shone clear as Heaven's gate.

And he these twain betwixt that rode
　　Was clad as white as wool,
Dyed in the Mercy of his God
　　White was he crown to sole.

Throned mid a myriad saints in bliss
　　Rise shall the Babe of Heaven
To shine on these three ghosts, iwis,
　　Smit thro' with sorrows seven.

Babe of the Blessèd Trinity
　　Shall smile their steeds to see:
Herod and Pilate riding by,
　　And Judas one of three.

A village under a starlit winter sky. Painting copyright Ideals Publications Incorporated.

The SEARCH

James Russell Lowell

I went to seek for Christ,
And Nature seemed so fair
That first the woods and fields my youth enticed,
And I was sure to find Him there:
The temple I forsook,
And to the solitude
Allegiance paid; but winter came and shook
The crown and purple from my wood;
His snows, like desert sands, with scorchful drift,
Besieged the columned aisle and palace gate;
My Thebes, cut deep with many a solemn rift,
But epitaphed her own sepulchered state!
Then I remembered whom I went to seek,
And blessed blunt winter for his counsel bleak.

So from my feet the dust
Of the proud World I shook;
Then came dear Love and shared with me His crust.
And half my sorrow's burden took.
After the World's soft bed,
Its rich and dainty fare,
Like down seemed Love's coarse pillow to my head,
His cheap food seemed as manna rare;
Fresh-trodden prints of bare and bleeding feet,
Turned to the heedless city whence I came,
Hard by I saw, and springs of worship sweet
Gushed from my cleft heart smitten by the same;
Love looked me in the face and spake no words,
But straight I knew those footprints were the Lord's.

I followed where they led,
And in a hovel rude,
With naught to fence the weather from His head,
The King I sought for meekly stood;
A naked, hungry child
Clung round His gracious knee,

And a poor hunted slave looked up and smiled
      To bless the smile that set him free;
New miracles I saw His presence do—
      No more I knew the hovel bare and poor,
The gathered chips into a woodpile grew,
      The broken morsel swelled to goodly store;
I knelt and wept: my Christ no more I seek,
His throne is with the outcast and the weak.

Painting by Frances Hook of a children's choir at candlelight service.
Painting copyright Ideals Publications Incorporated.

Christmas BELLS

Henry Wadsworth Longfellow

I heard the bells on Christmas Day
Their old, familiar carols play,
  And wild and sweet
  The words repeat
Of peace on earth, good-will to men.

And thought how, as the day had come,
The belfries of all Christendom
  Had rolled along
  The unbroken song
Of peace on earth, good-will to men!

Till, ringing, singing on its way,
The world revolved from night to day,
  A voice, a chime,
  A chant sublime
Of peace on earth, good-will to men!

And in despair I bowed my head;
"There is no peace on earth," I said;
  "For hate is strong,
  And mocks the song
Of peace on earth, good-will to men!"

Then pealed the bells more loud and deep:
"God is not dead; nor doth he sleep!
  The Wrong shall fail,
  The Right prevail,
With peace on earth, good-will to men!"

*The bells of a church in Warren, New Hampshire proclaim the message of
peace on earth to all mankind. Photograph copyright Johnson's Photography.*

Index